LLANWYNNO
a treasury of memories

~

ALAN J MEATS

LLANWYNNO
a treasury of memories

G2 rights ltd

G2 rights ltd

Llanwynno - A Treasury of Memories
Copyright ©Alan J Meats 2012

First edition published in the UK in September 2012
© G2 Rights Limited 2012
www.G2rights.co.uk

Print Edition ISBN: 978-1-78281-003-2

G2 Rights Ltd, Unit 9 Whiffens Farm, Clement Street, Hextable, Kent, BR8 7PG

LLANWYNNO
a treasury of memories

CONTENTS

INTRODUCTION

This book is a slightly abridged adaptation of the original volume that was published in Welsh in 1949 by Henry Lewis called 'Llanwynno' and translated the following year by Thomas Evans into English under the title, 'A History of Llanwynno'. Professor Lewis's book was based on a series of articles that appeared in an Aberdare periodical in the years leading up to 1887, the work of William Thomas, or Glanffrwd, as he was better known. As Henry Lewis says:

These essays describing Glanffrwd's native parish, Llanwynno, are not so much the history of a parish as a very graphic insight into the varied and colourful lifestyle of one of the large parishes in the county of Glamorgan when that lifestyle revolved around a thoroughly Welsh-speaking population. The writings of Glanffrwd certainly have their historical value, particularly as they present a warm-hearted, vibrant glimpse of both the working and leisure environment and also the gaiety of a society which Glanffrwd passionately loved. Here we have held before us characters, customs and pleasures; here superstitions and folk-lore abound; here appetites are whetted for the familiar industrial 'valleys' community to emerge by the end of the nineteenth century.

William Thomas, 'Glanffrwd', was born at Ynysybwl in 1843, the son of John Howell Thomas, the son of William Thomas Howell of Blaennantyfedw. He was a schoolmaster for five years before being called to the ministry of the Calvinistic Methodist Church, assuming the pastorate of Siloam, Gyfeillion, near Trehafod. Within a year he became a member of the Established Church and was ordained in 1875. He served his title in the parish of West Carnforth in Durham. From there he returned to Wales to be curate of Mold. Within 18 months he had been appointed Vicar-Choral of St Asaph in 1878 and Senior Vicar in 1888. Soon afterwards he fell victim to Parkinson's Disease and died on October 3rd. 1890. He was buried in Llanwynno Churchyard.

Three things acted as a spur to the composing of this book. Firstly, as someone nurtured in the area described by Glanffrwd but who subsequently headed west to taste life on the other side of the River Loughor, I find its contents have a special significance. Like Glanffrwd, recalling the impressions that his native area made on him in the 'foreign land of North-East Wales' where he died in 1890, I can identify with the 'exile writing of home'. Secondly, it would appear that the poetical, rather florid language the author uses (not surprisingly, since it dates from the end of the nineteenth century), needed to be simplified and made more reader-friendly for today's needs, without losing its 'romantic flavour'. Thirdly, and this is a purely personal motive, having tasted and been nourished by Glanffrwd's writings as a young student of the Welsh language,

I chose it as one of a series of books that were to make up the Archdeacon Lawrence Thomas Memorial Prize awarded me, to my eternal surprise, on completing my theological training.

Having retired as a parish priest of the Church in Wales in 2007 and reflecting on the countless services undertaken over years of public ministry, I can think of no greater service than the privilege of sharing the treasures of a parish dear to another priest of the Anglican church with as wide a readership as possible - whether they have, like me, a vested interest, or whether they simply join me in claiming that it is the inhabitants who truly bring to life the delights of describing any community.

The irony is there for all to see. Glanffrwd was brought up with the tide of radical non-conformity that swept South Wales at the time, but he transferred his allegiance from being a Free Church minister to seeking ordination into the Anglican church. He laments the destruction of the rural landscape and the blackening of the crystal-clear waters of his parish. In fact, were he alive today, he would be entranced to see that the pendulum has swung back and the verdant pastures he eulogised so nostalgically at the end of the nineteenth century have now become the 'green, green grass of home' of the early twenty-first century. How thrilled Glanffrwd would have been at this transformation and the return in many ways to 'what was'. Meanwhile, the characters who walk the stage of his writings, who, for me, impart the most precious of the treasures his memories offer, span the course of the centuries effortlessly.

May you be blessed as you read, or re-read, this fascinating 'little gem of social history', interwoven as it is with such a kaleidoscope of characters.

I record my sincere gratitude to Mr Brian Davies, Curator of Pontypridd Museum, for his encouragement in the producing of this book and for kindly providing the photographs contained within it, and to Pontypridd Town Library for their patience in dealing with a 'long-term' borrower.

I dedicate this book to the memory of all those I have had the privilege of knowing in the parishes in which I have served.

AJM

POSTSCRIPT: At the outset Glanffrwd asks the question, 'Who was Gwynno?' It has to be said that this Welsh saint certainly hid his light under a bushel! References to him are few and somewhat fragmented. I offer this brief piece of information. It seems from the famous medieval ecclesiastical document The Book of Llandaff that he was one of the five sons of Caio, whose name is commemorated in Cynwyl Gaio in Carmarthenshire. Gwynno's four brothers are given as Gwyn, Gwynoro, Celynin and Ceitho. The parish of Llanpumsaint in Carmarthenshire is so called because it is dedicated to the memory of all these five sons of Caio. The parish of Llantrisant in Glamorgan commemorates its three saints, Tyfodwg (retained in the parish name Ystradyfodwg in the Rhondda valley and often referred to by Glanffrwd), Illtyd, and, yes! - Gwynno. Most ancient calendars celebrate his Feast Day on November 1st (All Saints Day), one has it as 7 January.

Footnotes on the authors of the previous volumes published on this subject

HENRY LEWIS

Henry Lewis was Professor of Welsh at Swansea University from 1921 to 1954 and a Celtic scholar of distinction. The 'valleys' culture was very close to his heart. Having been brought up in the Swansea valley he married into a family from the Parish of Ystradyfodwg. His marital association with the Rhondda valley undoubtedly attracted him to the work of Glanffrwd. An eminent Celtic scholar, his prolific literary work included the editing of writings with a local interest such as 'A bailiff's companion' and 'The Glamorgan of Matthews Ewenni'.

THOMAS EVANS

Though his family originated in North Wales, Thomas Evans was born in Abercynon and became a schoolmaster. Having served on the staff of Abercynon Senior School he was appointed Headmaster of Abertâf Junior School in the Cynon valley. He was an ardent Welsh Baptist and an accomplished organist. Besides his 'History of Llanwynno' (a work of translation into English) he wrote two original books, 'The History of Abercynon' and 'The History of Miskin Higher or the Parishes of Llanwynno and Aberdare.'

ALAN J MEATS SERVED AS ASSISTANT PRIEST IN THE PARISH OF PONTYPRIDD, ST CATHERINE, WITH SPECIAL RESPONSIBILITY FOR THE COMMUNITY OF GLYNCOCH. HE WAS VICAR IN THE RECTORIAL BENEFICE OF YSTRADYFODWG AND A FORMER INCUMBENT OF ABERDARE, ST FAGAN. THESE PARISHES ARE PART OF, OR ADJACENT TO, THE ORIGINAL PARISH OF LLANWYNNO, DESCRIBED IN THIS BOOK. HE RETIRED FROM PARISH MINISTRY AS VICAR OF PENBRE WITH LLANDYRY IN 2007. HE WAS APPOINTED A RESIDENTIARY CANON OF ST DAVID'S CATHEDRAL IN 1994.

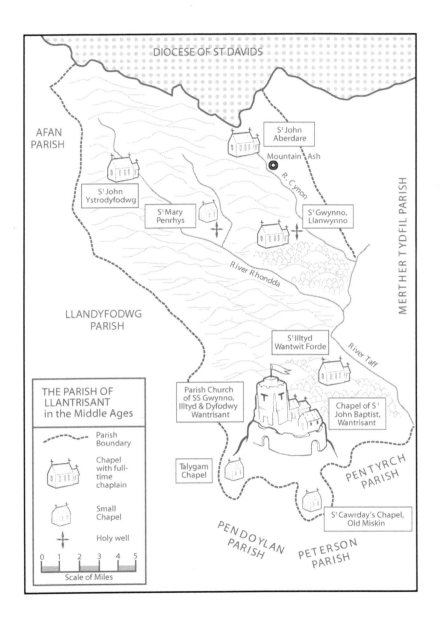

DIOCESE OF ST DAVIDS

AFAN
PARISH

St John
Aberdare

Mountain Ash

R. Cynon

MERTHER TYDFIL PARISH

St John
Ystrodyfodwg

St Mary
Penrhys

St Gwynno,
Llanwynno

River Rhondda

LLANDYFODWG
PARISH

St Illtyd
Wantwit Forde

River Taff

THE PARISH OF
LLANTRISANT
in the Middle Ages

Parish Church
of SS Gwynno,
Illtyd & Dyfodwy
Wantrisant

Chapel of St
John Baptist,
Wantrisant

- - - Parish
Boundary

Chapel
with full-
time
chaplain

Small
Chapel

Holy well

Talygam
Chapel

PENTYRCH
PARISH

0   1   2   3   4   5
Scale of Miles

St Cawrday's Chapel,
Old Miskin

PENDOYLAN
PARISH

PETERSON
PARISH

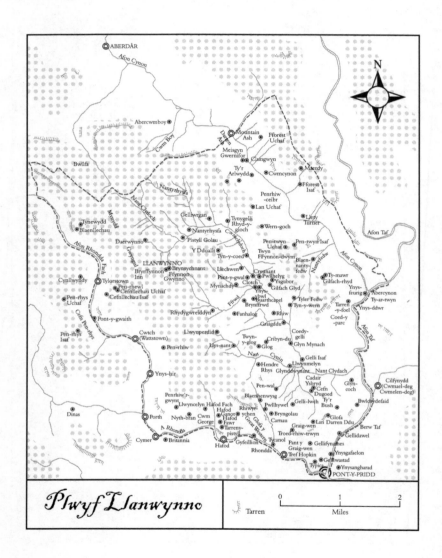

Plwyf Llanwynno

ABERDÂR

Afon Cynon

Abercwmboy

Cwm Boy

Abercwmboy

Bwllfa

DâR
Afon
Mountain
Ash

Fforest
Uchaf

Meisgyn
Gwernifor

Clungwyn

Maerdy

Ty'r
Arlwydd

Cwmcynon

Fforest
Isaf

Nantyrhysfa

Nant Clydach

Penrhiw
-ceibr

Lan Uchaf

Llety
Turner

Afon Taf

Gelliwrgan

Tynewydd
Blaenllechau

Nantyrhysfa

Tynygelli
Rhyd-y-
gloch

Wern-goch

Pistyll Golau

Pen-twyn
Uchaf

Pen-twyn Isaf

Daerwynno

Y Dduallt

Tyn-y-coed

Twyn
FFynnon-dwym

LLANWYNNO

Bryffynnon
Inn

Brynsychnant
FFynnon
Gwynno

Llechwen

Blaen-
nantyfedw

Nantyfedw

Ty-mawr
Gilfach-rhyd

Cynllwyndy

Tylorstown

Pen-rhewl
Cefnllechau Uchaf
Cefnllechau Isaf

Paut-y-gwal
Mynachdy

Clotch

Cromfant
Pwllhelyg

Ysgabor

Gilfach Glyd

Ynys-
feurig

Abercynon

Ty-ar-twyn

Pen-rhys
Uchaf

Pont-y-gwaith

Rhydygwreiddyn

Firwl
Ynys-
ybwl
Buarthcapel
Brynffrwd

Tyler Fedw
Tyn-y-wern

Tarren
-y-foel
Coed-y-
-parc

Ynys-ddwr

Pen-rhys
Isaf

Cwtch
(Wattstown)

Llwynperdid

Fanhaloc

Rhiw

Graigddu

Pen-rhiw

Llys-nant

Twyn-
y-glog

Cribyn-du

Glog

Coedy-
gelli
Glyn Mynach

Ynys-hir

Nant

Cynin

Gelli Isaf
Llwynmelyn

Penrhiw'r-
gwynt

Llwyncelyn

Hendre
Rhys

Glynddwynant

Nant Clydach

Dinas

Nyth-bran

Hafod Fach

Cwm
George

Pen-wal

Cadair
Ysbryd
Cefn
Dugoed

Glyn-
coch

Cilfynydd
(Cwmael-deg
Cwmelen-deg)

Porth

Afanod
ychen
Hafod
Fawr

Blaenhenwysg

Pwllhywel

Ty'r
Bush

Bwlchydefaid

A Rhondda

Tarren-
pistyll

Rhiwyr-
Glâs y
Great Western

Gelli-lwch

Graig-wen

Lan Darren Ddu

Glofa

Berw Taf

Cymer

Britannia

Hafod

Gyfeillion
Ty-canol
Rhondda

Troed-rhiw-trwyn

Pant y
Graig-wen

Gellidawel

Gellifynnes

Tref Hopkin

Ynysgafaelon
Gellwastad

Typica

Ynysangharad

PONT-Y-PRIDD

Plwyf Llanwynno

Tarren

0   1   2
Miles

CHAPTER ONE

LLANWYNNO AND ITS SURROUNDINGS

This book is made up of a series of articles on the history of Llanwynno that appeared in The Darian *newspaper, published in 1888 at Aberdare. The Llanwynno described in these pages derives from that period and the memory of the writer, William Thomas (Glanffrwd).*

It may be rightly said that this history lacks a certain chronology. This is explained by the fact that, as my mind returns to old Llanwynno, such a wealth of faces and events crowd in to my memory so easily that my imagination is fired at will by the very thought of them. Some prefer to write the name of the old parish in the Anglicised form, *'Llanwonno'*. The name of the saint who gives his name to the parish is Gwynno and not Gwonno, as these would have it. I say this because the saint was christened with the name Gwynno centuries before such misguided people were born! I well remember trying to dissuade the Llanwynno school governors from inserting 'Gwonno' as the spelling of the school logo which they proposed to adopt; the late John Andrew Wynn produced an old map of the parish showing this alleged 'correct' English spelling. However I happened to have an even older map on which could be

1

seen the name of the saint as 'Gwynno'. But whatever form the name took in the past, Llanwynno school had to have a fitting logo, and, unfortunately, its books, signs and stationery have stubbornly kept to the wrong name to this day!

Who was Gwynno? One of those ardent characters thrown up by the Welsh nation when they turned their backs on Druidism and paganism and embraced the faith of Jesus of Nazareth! There is no mention of his ever having performed miracles. No work of his has been preserved unless it is to be found in some old Latin book in the great Vatican library in Rome. As it is, only Gwynno's name remains with us. Not even the whereabouts of his grave are known. But the old church of Gwynno remains - Gwynno's Church - as the verse describes it:

'The ancient, notable church of Gwynno, built to offer such sweet and distinguished service to God with its clean floor as an offering on the altar of His praise'

The house of Daearwynno is not far from the old church. Gwynno probably lived in this farmhouse and may have owned the land around it, together with some part of Gwyngul Mountain, which he left either to the church or the poor of the parish; but this, like other matters, may have seen changes with the course of time. The fact is that it is significant that the nearest farmhouse to the church has always been known as 'Daearwynno', which means 'Gwynno's Land'. We are not told whether Gwynno the Saint, the church or the poor of the parish are the owners of the land. I do not think that a penny comes from the land of Daearwynno to help the poor of the parish. Five pounds a year from the nearby farm of Dduallt is shared among ten poor people who do not receive parish relief. The gift of ten shillings each is distributed on St Thomas's

Day in the porch of the church. I remember the time when there were not enough poor people to receive the money and the distributors had to search the parish for people who would be 'kind' enough to take the gift of ten shillings. Why St Thomas's Day for the sharing of this money? As it falls on December 21st, it is surely worth ten shillings to walk from anywhere in the parish to the church door on the shortest day of the year!

But lately the parish of Llanwynno has seen some big changes. The hustle and bustle, the hurry and scurry that have replaced the age-long peace and tranquillity are enough to cause Gwynno to rise in his grave and curse those who have broken the solitude of the parish and disturbed one of Nature's secluded spots. The Devil take it all!

The River Ffrwd mourns its lost purity and the River Clydach seems to want to run from its shame by hiding itself in the bosom of the River Taff. Dear Llanwynno, you have now been overtaken by the enemy! The sanctity of your beautiful fields has been trampled upon, your sweet-singing birds have been put to flight, the fiery steed has neighed and screamed like a thousand pigs through your lovely open spaces. So fair, so still, so pure, so tranquil, so dear were you before the adventurers burrowed through your very being! But now, you are well, like every other place where coal reigns. It is a pity there is no one adventurous enough to bring the sea to Ynysybwl! Yes, Ynysybwl is becoming a large and populous village alongside the River Clydach.

Down on the flat land below Ynysybwl you come to Glynmynach (The valley of the monk). The reason for its being named a valley is still obvious to the eye. Nothing is known of the monk. But it would not have been too much if the strangers and pilgrims had left the name alone, even if they failed to leave the land alone. The old name 'Glynmynach' brings to mind many thoughts, whispers of years gone by. It smacks of a special period in our history seen right before our eyes just like many an old house found in a town can show the new houses that something worthwhile had been there before them. But Glynmynach has gone, or at least has been changed. Robertstown, if you please! Yes, Robert's Town. What an insult! There is no charm, beauty, character or dignity in the name, and it is in English too. We are grateful for that. The Welsh form of it, namely Tref Robert, would have been awful! The place was once called Black Rock. A new house was built and it was named Glynmynach. This house still stands, but it is now one of the houses of Robert's Town, if you please! Soon we shall have an English corruption of the River Clydach! Commerce at its worst is heartless. It knows nothing of love of country, love of language, nor love of hill and vale. 'Coal, iron, gold, silver' is its language. So it is that the old parish of Gwynno has come under a new stewardship. A few years ago one could count the souls of the parish from the top of Cefn Gwyngul mountain to the foot of Graig yr Hesg, and from the banks of the Taff and Cynon to the banks of the River Rhondda in Blaenllechau and Ystrad; but now, even Ynysybwl has become an anthill and the ancient but somewhat crude prophecy about the place has come true:

'Ynysybwl, that picturesque settlement on lush pasture, a dreamy place on the river bank. An angel of man's creation will come and tear it apart.'

Well well! Ynysybwl, as it was, is dear to me. Llanwynno, as it was before the smoke of the train darkened it, is dear to me. That is how I remember it - my old playground! The land of the 'hop, step and jump' of my childhood; I would give much to have you as in those far off days, but 'yesterday will never return for anyone'.

In the next chapters I shall return to the old names and characters which my love and memory connect with Llanwynno. Here are some of them: Rhys and Als; Tom the Cobbler; Tommy of Penrhiw; Edwards of Gilfachglyd; old Williams of Gellilwch; the hermit of Glan Elai; Billy and Jennie of Llysnant; Dewi Haran: Evans of Mynachdŷ; Ieuan the son of Iago; Evan Moses and other old inhabitants, who were never out of sight of the chimney smoke of Llanwynno, yet they have made their mark and managed to humour us.

CHAPTER TWO

THE HILLS

There is something poetic in the landscape around Llanwynno, with all its rich variety. Take a walk from Pontypridd through the heart of the parish towards Aberdare and many a fair corner and handsome view will cry out for attention. Take Graig yr Hesg near the old town of Pontypridd. The people should be proud of it. Its stark, threatening appearance in winter is grand and majestic; and in the spring sunshine when verdure and growth creep over the old grey stones, and when all the trees are decked with the green mantle of life, oh! it is then poetry itself, with the Berw section of the Taff like a lake of pure inspiration seething and ever whispering at its foot. There is no need to go to Scotland or to Switzerland to see romantic scenery. So you are close to Graig yr Hesg and the Berw of the Taff and then, if you go to the top of the Graig hill, you will see one of the grandest views ever - the Taff valley below stretching before you as if inviting you to Cardiff through meadows that are like the garden of the Lord; the side of Eglwysilan mountain like one of the walls of Nature intent on protecting the valley; the farmhouses like hayricks of lime making the slopes sparkle; the spirit of poetry moving at will on the summit, while the precipices set the heart alight. Go more often to the top of Graig yr Hesg, you people of Pontypridd; you will enjoy scenery that will surely soothe the spirit and sharpen the appetite for dinner as well!

A little further on, nearer to the heart of the parish, you reach the foot of the Glôg. One is inclined to consider it an artificial mound, but not so. It is too splendid to be the work of man's polluted hand. It is so round, isn't it? It is like a great marble covered with grass and the sheep decking its slopes and summit. It is Nature's own work. There are old grey stones peeping out through the trees, and from its side ice-cold waters are distilled, as pure as heaven and as delicious as the nectar of the gods. The old mound to me is like the birthplace of magic, and it is difficult for me to compose a piece of poetry or draw any kind of imaginative picture without the Glôg crowding in to it. I don't suppose the railway, the coal and smoke will come to poison the old Mound now, having already stretched their tendrils into the heart of the parish. If they do, it will be an act of sacrilege and the gravest of sins.

Going on a bit higher through the parish, one comes to Foelyddduallt (the summit of the dark slope). This summit is not as attractive as the Glôg, but it has a wildness and beauty of its own. The impression it made on me as a child was that it was trying to peep over the ridge of Ffynnon-dwym and Werngoch in order to catch a glimpse of another old hill whose feet were planted in the River Cynon. Moelydduarth has been a place for testing coal levels since time immemorial. Many holes can be seen in its sides. People of old would make a hole and perhaps dig out some coal, but when they saw the light of day fading as they went in, they would start another coal level, until the hill became pitted with holes; but it still stood firm. Hywel Ddu had dug holes there and had succeeded in penetrating further under its roots than any predecessor. When I last saw the hill, Hywel had put up a tent in the shelter of the land where he was digging and I noticed that he had pitched his tent exactly on the same spot where the old people used to see a spirit called the Ghost of Ysgubor Clun. Presumably he had gaslight there. It worried the old inhabitants for a long time and they spoke of it with dread. In their innocence they did not know the difference between the light blue flame of gas and the spirit of some wretch who had hanged himself on one of the trees of Coed y Foel.

Old Vicar Jones tried to exorcise the spirit and solemnly warn him to wait a thousand years in order to carry water from the Red Sea in a sieve, and having finished that task, to make a rope damp with sea sand to be given to the parishioners as a bell-rope for Gwynno's church. This is how one old poet wrote of this spirit and of others in the district:

A ghost lives on Cefn yr Erw(at the rear of the land), of a wretch who cut his throat, and a ghost who inhabits Ysgubor y Clun (Barn in the meadow), that of a miser who killed himself.

Not far from the Dduallt, but somewhat behind it, the traveller reaches Pistyll Golau (The Fountain of Light). This is a very lovely waterfall which tumbles down into quite a low glen. Above it are Gwyngul Mountain and the old parish church, the resting place for so many of Llanwynno's residents. The ancient church and its sacred churchyard nestle under a rocky escarpment that juts out rather suddenly from the old mountain. What a peaceful spot! Imagine the wind forever roaring or whispering on the summit or in the lee of the mountain without the fumes of engine or the clang of hammer; only the feet of traveller or the shepherd's whistle to disturb the tranquillity and silence of this old burial place on the mountain slope. The Pistyll intones its bass notes as it flows in the depth of the glen, and the sound of this waterfall is in harmony with the spirit of he who stands here looking down on the land of slumber of so many generations of Llanwynno people. Here lie the remains of many who lost their lives in more than one explosion in the Blaenllechau (top of the slates) pits. The soft breeze of Gwyngul mountain sings a requiem as they pass over them, while the Pistyll in the valley below plays a majestic accompaniment as it rolls down over the ridge to froth and foam like a miniature Niagara. What amusement the old people caused when giving names to places! And they were always apt! How true to life and descriptive is the name Pistyll Golau. Down in a dark hole in the glen under the branches of stout oaks and brushwood, the waterfall is white and frothy, lighting up the whole of the nook when in full flow and fullest vigour, completely fulfilling its name.

We have now reached wild mountain land and the traveller can say, like the goat, 'Give me the freedom of countryside and mountain'.

Within sight is Fforch-don, and the River Clydach sets out on its journey like a shaft of light surfacing among turf and peat but soon expanding to a silver ribbon, rolling on towards Cardiff. Again the name Fforch-don (fork in the land) is very descriptive. The land forks its way upward on to the green mountain ridge; this is smooth and fair pasture land, not wet and marshy. North Walians never use the word 'ton' meaning 'virgin soil'. It is difficult sometimes to get them to understand its meaning, but it is often on the lips of those brought up in Glamorgan.

It is hardly worth turning back now without a climb up Mynydd Bach (Little Mountain) from where we are afforded a grand view of the Cynon valley from Mountain Ash up to Hirwaun. The town of Aberdare does not look as handsome today as it did to the shepherds of Mynydd Bach two hundred years ago, before the coal-tips scarred the face of the parish. Today, nothing but coal, smoke, steam, and a general blackness greets the eye of the beholder from the top of Mynydd Bach and he feels it time to turn back to gaze at the green fields of the old parish, threatened by the same fate. We leave the Cynon down on our left, like a snake which has defiled itself in the coal-dust of the Dyffryn (the Valley) and we walk to the top of the ridge above with our faces set towards Pontypridd, but on the east of the valley, leaving Ynysybwl in a bowl in the heart of the countryside. We are now on Tarren y Foel or Foel y Gelli (The summit of the grove). Below we see that quaint little village called Navigation, formerly the Basin, and before that Ynysfeurug (now Abercynon). It is also called Aberdare Junction. These English names have sat uncomfortably on the place. I think the intention is to restore the Welsh name, as the school is mentioned as Ynysfeurug School.

I could say many things about the place, but I must be content with one rather personal note. My grandfather, William Thomas Howell, had a lease on land in Ynysfeurug drawn up in the old-fashioned Welsh way - to last while water flowed in the River Cynon and as long as he paid £4 rent per annum. Poor chap! He was fond of his pint, and one day, under its influence, he sold the lease to someone for £20. When I now pass through the place, seeing everything in the hands of strangers, I find it an effort to say, 'Bless the old man who played such a trick on his descendants. But I must be like the maidservant of Tydraw who spilt a bucket of milk on the floor and consoled herself with the thought that it was impossible to put it back again. It's no use crying over spilt milk.'

But here we are on the summit of Tarren y Gelli. On one side flows the Taff, on the other the Clydach, and between the two are a thousand delights. Here we have the huntsman's paradise. Many a time have I hunted a fox here and often have I heard the sides of the Darren split open with the endless cry of the 'Tally-Ho!

Tarren y Foel and Penparc Woods are the home of the Glamorgan foxes. The inhabitants of Llanwynno have always been eager for the hunt from their youth and even today you will see among them many a hardy Nimrod. The 'wow' of the huntsman, the hunting–call of the Glôg, the melodious baying of the hounds, are still to be heard in Llanwynno, while the hare calls the place his own in the Gelli fields and Reynard takes his pick of the feathered fare in Tarren y Foel till the present day.

CHAPTER THREE

YNYSBWL, THE VILLAGE AND SOME
OF ITS CHARACTERS

It is likely that Ynysybwl will become a large and populous place. Already its appearance has changed and before long the transformation will be so great that no trace of the quiet, peaceful village known as Ynysybwl will be with us.

I mentioned that it is situated in a deep hollow, with the hills surrounding it on all sides. The sun has to rise quite high before it touches the lowest part of the valley. The hill of Maes y Gaer (The Field of the Fort) and the slopes of Tyle'r Fedw (The Hill of the Birch Trees) and the Gelli shelter it from the keen easterly winds. On the west side stands Buarth y Capel (Chapel Farmyard) and higher still Fanheulog (Sunny Place), while climbing still further we arrive at Mynydd Gwyngul; between that mountain and landmarks to the north we see the lands of Mynachdy (Monastery) and the Dduallt, both on fairly high ground. Thus the ancient village of Ynysybwl nestled in the sheltered base of the valley, while the River Clydach flowed quietly under the protecting slopes; the Ffrwd for its part rushes down to meet her, wilder in temperament due to its being upset by the mill, the rocks and the falls around it. Here in Ynysybwl the rivers Clydach and Ffrwd meet, flowing as one until swallowed by the River Taff near Glyncoch, now almost within sight of Pontypridd. Older people considered the Taff a big and dangerous river, due to the abrupt rise in its flow after the rains and heavy thunderstorms of the upland area. One of the old poets of the parish wrote of the Taff thus:

'The Taff is a passionate, awesomely turbulent river; it has carried a hundred lives away and follows a terrifying course.'

Now that the Taff has taken the life of the Clydach, let us leave her and return to Ynysybwl as she was in the days of her former peace and natural tranquillity, not as now, rudely awakened by the steam engine, trampled on, defiled and deprived of her glory, destroyed, her poetic nature swallowed up without conscience and her fair beauty bowed low. You villain! I can hardly refrain from cursing you for coming so near to the quiet homes of the birds, fish and hares that mark the area between the Ffrwd and the Clydach. It is so easy to destroy, but it takes divine power to create. Nobody can ever make Ynysybwl the place it once was. Oh no!

'Humpty Dumpty sat on the wall, Humpty Dumpty had a great fall; all the King's horses and all the King's men couldn't put Humpty Dumpty on the wall again.'

Perhaps Nature and its geographical situation have given Ynysybwl its name. However it seems natural to call it Ynys y Pwll ('Island in the Pool'). In English it is called Bowling Green. I don't know who anglicised the name but there is no doubt that such a person is wrong. The place was called Ynys y Pwll long before it was called Bowling Green. The name Ynys y Pwll has continued since time immemorial, but fairly recently a form of the French game 'boules' has been introduced, to give it the Welsh 'bŵl'. Therefore I owe thanks to nobody for giving an English name to the place! Eventually Ynysybwl became the name of the whole district, up to the Parish Houses and all surrounding areas.

It is said that the antiquarian Camden, the Strabo of England, as he is called, once paid a visit to Ynysybwl when gathering material for his history, *Britannia*, and that he slept a night here, no doubt in the Old Inn. Camden was a very learned man and had made a study of Gaelic, Welsh and Old English to equip him for his work. His first book, *Britannia*, was published in 1586, and his second work, *Anglicana Normanica Cambrica*, in 1603. I am inclined to believe that it was for this latter work that he visited Ynysybwl and that his main purpose was to see the monastery, Mynachdy.

The monastery had been dissolved in the reign of Henry VIII, 40 or 50 years before Camden's visit. One wonders what became of the books and the history of the place. Mynachdy was a very fine farmhouse when Camden visited it; the monks and others who lived there had been dispossessed of their abode, some to various stations in life, others being 'called home' to the churchyard of Gwynno.

I shall have more to say again about Mynachdy. I must leave it now with rather a personal note. When Mynachdy was dissolved, two monks, who were brothers, lived there. They were Hywel, son of Hywel, and Llewelyn, son of Hywel. My family, the Howells of Cwmcynon, and the family of Llewelyn of the Forest Farm, are descendants of these two brothers. When they were dispossessed from Mynachdy , they married two sisters, and I think that Hywel (from whom I am descended) spent his life in the Cynon valley and that Llewelyn (whose descendents adopted his Christian name) lived on the slopes of the Forest and somewhere else in Breconshire. However the Howells lived long and owned the land from Abercynon to Upper Cwmcynon, near Mountain Ash.

We have wandered from Ynysybwl, so we now return.

An annual fair was instituted in Ynysybwl; how long ago I have not been able to find out yet, but it was very famous. People came from many distances and animals from surrounding areas were brought to be bought and sold. In fact in one fairly old almanac it is called 'The Buying and Selling Fair of Ynyspool' to distinguish it from a purely pleasure fair. It was held on March 16th, and apart from business, much fighting occurred. Here the muscle and skill of the younger generation of the parish were tested. Here was decided whether the men of Ynysybwl, Blaenllechau or the Rhondda Fach were the strongest. Here the feud between the men of Llanfabon and Llanwynno was settled, and often the men of Llanwynno had an old score to pay back on those of Llantrisant. These matters were well and truly sorted on the night of the fair.

Several families took Fair night as an opportunity to give expression to their own 'local difficulties'. When the boys of Llwynperdid had a couple of black eyes each and noses like sheep's heads, and the Dduallt boys were almost minus their noses apart from two or three broken ribs, they all went home satisfied and peace would break out for another year. Arrangements were also made at the Fair for the hay-cutting competition in the summer and the annual race of one mile on Mynydd Gwyngul, from a point called Heol-las upwards. Races had taken a strong hold on the parish since the days of Gruffydd Morgan or Guto Nythbrân, the fastest and lightest on foot this country has ever seen. We will talk about him later on.

Many cattle drovers came to Ynysybwl Fair, often arriving the night before, and many a practical joke was played on them by the local people, for Ynysybwl folk were noted for fun and their skill in playing handball, bando and wrestling. There was just the right place for this in Ynysybwl. Here was the most notable playing field in the country; the Cae Bach y Fedw (The Little Birch Field) and the meadows from the Ynys down to the Pandy (the Fulling Mill) were ideal for playing bando and football.

In Ynysybwl there lived a well-known shopkeeper and his wife, named Rhys Dafydd and Als, or, as he was often called, 'Als the wife of Rhys, the husband of Als.' They kept a shop in a small house where Aberffrwd now stands. Rhys and Als were a quaint couple and so was their shop. The whole stock consisted of about two pounds of candles and a few other useful little things. Half a crown would have bought the lot! And yet Als was so afraid of the shop catching fire that she refused to sell matches when they first came out.

Rhys was a rather tall man, rather rough in appearance. He was a thorough Welshman, with a rustic appearance and the definite ways of Ynysybwl about him. He was quite inoffensive, except when he and Als had an occasional row because of her pig-headedness, he alleged, but in my opinion because of her naivety. One big quarrel they had once about the moon. Als had got up early one morning, and looking out, saw the moon just on the wane. She took it to be a new moon and told her husband so. Matters came to a head with Rhys saying as a parting shot,

'Whoever heard of a new moon in the morning?' Als replied,

'I saw it with my own eyes, so mud be in your eyes, Rhys Dafydd!'

Neither of them got the upper hand. Rhys went back to his cobbling and Als to weighing a halfpenny worth of snuff for Mari Rhys from the New Houses.

The next quarrel was about dividing a pound of candles into two half-pounds. One evening a servant from Ffynnondwym (Hot Fountain) called for a pound of candles, which happened to be seventeen candles. The problem was too much for Als, as she couldn't for the life of her divide the pound into two equal parts. Rhys too was nonplussed. He wanted to put eight in half and nine in the other, but Als thought that this was unfair and one–sided. She decided to cut one candle in half, putting eight and a half in each packet. In cutting the candle with Rhys's cobbler's knife, it broke into several little pieces! From then on they decided to sell the candles at a halfpenny each or by the whole pound. Rhys was in a bad temper for days. I remember hearing of Als walking to Pentwyn to buy a pig, a whole pig. When she arrived there she said that Rhys had sent her to buy the pig and to offer 5s 6d, but if she couldn't get it for 5s. 6d. to offer six shillings. Naturally the Pentwyn people preferred six shillings to 5s 6d!

Als once paid a visit to Tynewydd (New House) in the month of June and she looked forward to having festival cake for tea. She had tea and cake but not the special festive cake. After drinking her cup of tea, she tossed the dregs over her shoulder on to the carpet. The lady of the house gave a meaningful hint that there was a basin for the deposit of tea leaves on the table, but Als would respond to no hints. She insisted that it was more convenient to dispatch them on to the carpet because there was more room for them there; the remains of four good black cups of tea rested that night on the Tynewydd carpet. Poor Als! So innocent, so simple, and yet how happy was her lot. She had a wide knowledge of herbs and plants, how to gather and dry them, how to use them in case of illness. I remember her giving medicinal wormwood tea to Mocyn, the cat, whose appetite had started to fail. The cause of the loss of appetite was probably due to his having eaten too many rabbits! However every spring he had to endure the same treatment! Some say that the cat had to be given brimstone and treacle in the autumn to purify his blood. Rhys knew nothing about this. Perhaps some mischievous boys had put the story about!

Her mind was full of old memories and events involving people of yesteryear. Her mind overflowed with the existence of spirits. She firmly believed that they did the rounds of the place, especially on New Year's Eve, when they were to be seen on every path in the country. Als suffered many a fright and a great deal of bother with the spirit that haunted the gate of Cae'r Defaid (Sheep Field). This was the spirit that had assured her that other spirits existed. Nobody can know what the poor old woman went through with this spirit, but it had taken the form of a donkey, and even brayed like a donkey; in a word, he behaved like an ass in the darkness under the branches of a big oak tree in Cae'r Defaid. As there was a savagely ill-tempered donkey in Mynachdy at that time that had been seen by people near the spot where Als had seen the spirit, and since this same donkey was in the habit of frightening the people of nearby houses, many thought that he must have been the spirit that Als saw on returning from Gelliwrgan. This was when the darkness got the better of her and put the wind up her. But she continued to believe that a spirit lived there and, for that matter, still lives there.

So far I have stressed Als's failings. But given her lack of knowledge and her simplicity, she possessed certain virtues and in her own way she was a clever old woman. She died in ripe old age. I was a small lad when she died but I remember her quite well. I have good cause to remember the stick that she used for support as she walked about the district. Many a time the end of it landed on my head rather heavily. I will not reveal why I received those blows! Poor Als and Rhys now lie by Gwynno's church and their earthly tabernacle has long become one with the soil of Mynydd Gwyngul.

I rather believe that Rhys was a native of Llantwit Major and that Als first saw the light of day at Ystrad Rhondda. They were good, peaceful neighbours and if their weaknesses caused some people to smile, their innocence and other virtues caused those who knew them best to love and respect them. Their behaviour and appearance were typically Welsh. Fashion passed them by. They wore black woollen stockings and home-spun clothes, designed in the most rustic fashion possible and yet they always looked spick and span. I think that the old Welsh manner of dress, language and customs is far superior to that of today. I don't think Als knew a word of English, though Rhys may have spoken a little. Apart from a slight encroachment, English in those days had not penetrated beyond Pontypridd. I would venture to say that it is a pity it ever came at all! I love to hear about you carefree, single-minded, monoglot people of Llanwynno and I salute your memory.

CHAPTER FOUR

THE SEARCH FOR COAL AND LIME

For many years people had encroached upon the banks of the Ffrwd on the south side of Mynachdy in their search for coal. The old level is still partly open and coal is worked from the same vein lower down the river bank by Mr Daniel Thomas of Pontypridd. The old level was but a narrow hole, with scarcely enough room for a donkey and its load to come through, but many a load managed to come out to keep the people of the Cwm and the hillsides warm during the cold, cruel winters. My grandfather had a lease on the coal until the late Mr Evans sold it to Alaw Goch of Ynyscynon (later of Miskin). No coal was worked from this level after the land was sold until it was reopened by the Bard from Aberdare, when tools such as mandrels, shovels, hammers, wedges, lamps and oil-vessels were discovered. These items had been there for twenty years, more or less, without anyone ever having seen them, except for my grandfather's spirit.

In this level they worked a donkey that attracted more attention than any of his long-eared brethren. He was known for miles around, and since people from the hills, the Ffaldau, Bwllfa, Maerdy and other remote places came to the level for coal, the donkey's fame had spread far and wide. He was the most infamous donkey I ever saw. He had many a hiding from my grandfather for doing things that nobody thought a donkey would ever dream of doing. Often on a Monday morning when Dick the donkey was due to 'clock in' at the level, he was nowhere to be found. He would have gone 'visiting' on a Sunday, taking great care not to return in time for work. Another time I saw him hiding for days in the undergrowth near the level, when nobody thought he was anywhere near, while everyone in the parish was searching for him. No donkey, no coal! Dick knew from experience what lay in store for him. Morgan Jones's lambasting of the donkey had been prepared. But the effort of getting within striking distance of Dick had to be achieved. The battle in the wood between donkey and master was long and fierce. You could not see them, but you could hear the 'slash, slash,' a shouted curse, a loud 'hee, haw, haw' and a wild gallop through thorns and undergrowth with another chase through the trees on the river bank. After a time the battle would end and peace would reign, But woe betide anyone who tried to interfere. Nobody dared say anything bad about the donkey to Morgan but I don't think Dick ever had an atom of respect for anyone on earth except perhaps for Morgan Jones.

I well remember a couple of the old donkey's wicked tricks. One of the residents -Dafydd Rhys by name - had come to help cut coal for a week or a fortnight in winter when the demand was greatest. One day Dafydd had started out with Dick and the tram early in the afternoon. Morgan Jones had told them to go while it was still light. They went off amiably enough. Dafydd Rhys took his dinner of bread and cheese and Dick some of the hay in the lodge. After eating and resting a while, they prepared to re-enter the level. Dafydd, however, observed signs of unwillingness in the vicinity of Dick's ears. He approached the animal warily, intending to grab him by the head and guide him into starting his underground journey. Dick's ears bent down, his hair stood on end like the mane of a fierce lion and pitched battle commenced. Dafydd was first to touch the ground with Dick trying his best to get the boot in. Dafydd shouted the place down. The fracas lasted an hour or more while Dafydd bled freely from his injuries. In the end help came and Dick was persuaded to start again for the coal-face, where Morgan Jones was waiting for them. In they went but no sign of them could be seen of them reaching the far end.

Morgan, tired of waiting, thought it wise to start looking for them. When he had gone a short distance he found them in a most distressed condition. Dafydd had got out of the dram to open the door through which they had to enter. Dick saw his chance, and as Dafydd passed alongside him, Dick squeezed him hard against the side of the level, so that he could not move either way. He was like a helpless slab of cake and, to make matters worse, his lamp had gone out! When Morgan reached the spot, Dafydd had gone blue in the face and could scarcely breathe. Dafydd's opinion of Dick was summed up many times in these words: 'I don't think he's a donkey at all, he can't possibly be; I think he's the Old Nick himself, indeed I do.'

Another of Dick's nasty tricks was when he attacked the old mare of Llysnant (the Manor by the Stream). Billy of Llysnant had come for a bag of coal, but as he was early, he let the old mare off to graze. She was a bit long in the tooth too! In a while the sound of wheels was heard and Dick's ears appeared. The load of coal was brought to the loading point, Dick was released and the men went to fill the bag of coal. The donkey had seen the old mare enjoying some of his hay on the other side of the lodge. He went straight up to her and grabbed her nose with his teeth; a battle royal erupted, with the old mare screaming like a pig under the butcher's knife. As she kicked and bit with all her might, Billy rushed over to help her, poor chap, and an even fiercer battle was waged between Dick and Billy. Billy fell over the edge into the brook and Dick raised his forefeet on to Billy's shoulders. His yell as he landed on his face in the stream was terrifying. 'Stop, you white-nosed devil, stop!' he shouted, while the onlookers were too beside themselves with laughter to help him, even though Billy was in some danger. The row ended with Dick having the beating of his life and Billy saying, 'What's the good of that? His hide is as thick as the devil's.'

No doubt these things will sound very silly to some people, but to those who remember that period, this incident will bring back memories of amusing events, such as this, that were part of the scene at Mynachdy Level. Dick's fame was so great in the parish that it is only fair to give some account of his life. Nobody knew his age but he must surely have been a patriarch among the donkey clan. In his old age he was sold to work in one of the pits at Cefnpennar.

What became of him, poor old Dick? William of Tynywern, and Dick had slept many a night in the lodge. William wrote a verse or two occasionally. He wrote Dick's epitaph, although I believe that Will died before Dick in the end and the graves of both have sunk into oblivion. Here is the epitaph:

'I've never seen a donkey so temperamentally bad,
He bit and kicked throughout his life, his tribe even deemed him mad.
If ever he does pass away, the stupid feckless sinner,
May Llantwit's fleas devour his skin, his carcase the crows' dinner.'

We had a lot of fun when we congregated at the Level. People from distant corners of the parish met there and related all the local history; stories were told, songs were sung and verses were recited by the lodge fire. It was a regular meeting place and, on the whole, all were the better for it. The period of the pack-ponies was a happy one. Even if it was an inconvenient method of transport, I am sure it suited those days just as today's mode of transport suits these days.

Another meeting point was the lime kiln. I remember hearing the sound of horses' hoofs passing by very early at a certain time of the year. Daearwynno's horses were in the care of Siôn Arnold. There were some from Blaenllechau and Ffynnon-dwym, usually three or four pack-horses in charge of one man. They made for Ynysdwr Kiln, between the Bridge and the Basin, or to Gwernygerwn Kiln, near Trefforest, for lime. There was often a lot of excitement, when the River Taff was in flood; there was no bridge, only a ford, to reach Ynysdwr from Llanwynno.

I remember a big flood once when Ffynnondwym's horses were crossing at the ford. The bags fell off and burnt in the water, while Morgan Morgan was nearly drowned! The horses managed to cross over somehow, but Morgan was left stranded. Eventually he was released from his perilous position!

Liming time meant early rising. In the remote parts of the parish they were up soon after midnight and by the time they caught the horses and fixed them and their saddles securely, stopping to enjoy a good dishful of bread soaked in milk, it was time to start for the kilns. There were many amusing incidents and much hearty laughter as they came down from Blaenllechau and Daearwynno, sometimes at an easy pace, sometimes at a quick trot, occasionally at a wild gallop, all depending on the mood of men and horses. On one occasion they roared with laughter when they gave a lift to old Ifan Morgan who was crossing the mountain, only for the horse to break into a headlong gallop, while Ifan clung with one hand to the horse's mane and the other to the saddle, shouting, 'Wo, Wat! Wo, Wat! Gwellti!'

This method of fetching lime has passed out of fashion now and few remember the old pack-ponies. The cart or trolley came into use, which was much more convenient, but not half as Welsh or as romantic as the old 'packs'. In becoming more advanced we lose originality; by becoming fashionable we lose a certain homeliness, and in becoming less homely we lose much of the notoriety and humour of the upland area.

I remember the great stir brought about when wool was taken from Llanwynno to the Fulling Mill at Machen, which was the home of the poet Gwilym Ilid. The wool from the farms was brought down to the Lower Barn and from there it was taken in Mynachdy's big wagon, with a cart or two as well. During the day it was packed into a big load, and some time during the night, the journey to Machen would begin. In the company would travel many of the quaint old farmers of the parish astride their ponies. Among them would some well known characters like Walter of Nantyrysfa, Evan from Daearwynno, Twmi of Mynachdy, Dafydd from the Dduallt, Siencyn from Gelliwrgan, Tomos of Blaenllechau. In this rural pilgrimage to Machen there would often be some adventure, sometimes of a serious nature, but more often, humorous.

In those times there was much talk of hypnotism, then quite a novel thing. There were one or two men at the Pandy in Machen who claimed to have the power of hypnotising people. Walter Nantyrysfa decided to give the hypnotist a trial with regard to the painless extraction of a tooth that had been giving him trouble for a long time. The man thought he had put Walter to sleep, so slipping his fingers into Walter's mouth, he touched the aching tooth. Walter's teeth closed fast on the hypnotist's fingers. Although the man howled piteously, Walter would not let go. It is still not known exactly who was mesmerised, Walter or the man. There were more traces of Walter's teeth on the man than there were of hypnotism on Walter!

Walter was a short, round, portly man, always riding a little Welsh pony; many a time, very early in the morning. I sat behind him on the pony on the wild mountain top to the edge of Aberaman woods, in the summer abode of sheep and lambs. Walter would often dismount and catch a lamb with the aid of the dog, and if it suffered from some kind of ailment, he would spit tobacco juice into its eye. I was scarcely eight years old when I went on these wanderings with Walter. But every trip and every scene of those happy days are still alive in my memory. Allow me to end this chapter with a verse or two to Walter and the old farmers as a small tribute:

'You kindly people of the wild hills, I love to remember your adventures pursuing the cattle, lambs and sheep through sun, rain and wind.
You had little education but your knowledge of nature was great, The signs of the sun, the look of the sky, the murmur of springs on the slopes.'
These signs you understood, you could foretell the weather, seeing the mist on the hill-top or the little stream flowing like wine,
You were innocent and free, Llanwynno was your heaven before the smoke defiled the day and the breezes of your hills.
Rest and sleep in the good earth is what you loved throughout your days, In spite of smoke and all it means, Mount Gwyngul's zephyrs still smell sweet.

May the breeze carry its murmur above your graves beside the church and, when my term on earth is spent, to Gwynno's church may I be sent.'

CHAPTER FIVE

OLD CUSTOMS

Another old custom that brought the people of the parish nearer together was the system of 'Free Help' or 'Act of Neighbourliness.' People came to help with the hay, the ploughing, the reaping, etc. They came from far and near to show their neighbourliness in this way. The 'Cymorth', as it was called by the locals, always had its fun and disputes. There was always great rivalry in the way all helped with the haymaking to see who had the distinction of being 'top dog' at cutting the hay in the widest, most even and neatest strokes. There would be much judging and conferring about the swathes of hay, the edge of the scythe and the position of the cutter. One was deemed to have a good edge to his scythe but his bearing was questionable. Someone else was too round backed; he would never be skilful with the scythe because his buttocks were too long! One may be deficient in cutting in the open field while another may fail the test when cutting by the hedge. One man of great experience usually escaped all these faults and he would be selected as champion for the season.

Many had such high opinions of father, brother or friend that they would not consider conferring the accolade on anyone else. Such a person was Iantws from the Llechwen, for whom no one was equal to the task like his brother Rhys. Rhys had been a champion in his day, but now was old and weak. 'Who is going to win at the Llechwen Cymorth today, Iantws?' called a friend one day, when poor old Rhys was too old to wield a scythe at all. 'Oh! Rhys, my brother, of course,' answered Iantws.

These gatherings were of great benefit in many ways. The parishioners were drawn together and had an opportunity to show their regard for friends and show their skill as haymakers and reapers. Well-known fields for such purpose were the nine-acre and seven-acre fields of Ffynnondwym, the nine-acre and five-acre fields of Gilfachyrhydd, the seven-acre field of Tyle'r fedw, the fields of Coedcae'r Gwair (Trees by the Hayfield) and Gwaun y Castell (Castle Meadow) of Mynachdy, as well as the moors of Dduallt and Darwynno. I could relate many incidents and amusing stories about these but not to go into too much detail I mention only some of the most famous haymakers of the parish who have put away their scythes, spades and mattocks and gone to rest after their hard day's rest until the ridge of the church will free itself from its foundations at the resounding trumpet-call of the Archangel when 'time shall be no more.'

In his day Evan Rhys, the father of the poet Merfyn, was considered a champion haymaker. My father, John Thomas, one of the sons of Blaen Nant y Fedw, was the strongest and fastest in his day, and Mr Evans, Mynachdy, also had a good name for cutting hay. He often boasted that he could cut an acre of hay and shear a hundred sheep in the same day. His brother, William, was good when he tried, but he was seldom on his best form. Evan Jenkins, Tyle'r Fedw, was also considered an expert with the scythe; but why name any more? The parish reared strong, stalwart men and it would be difficult to find their equal anywhere, whether it was at haymaking, reaping, playing ball, fox-hunting, or anything else they undertook.

I remember one haymaking Cymorth when Tom the blacksmith was asked to gather up the hay and later invited to dinner. Many still remember Tom. You could not wish for a more shapely body than his. He was like a handsome, round oak tree growing in the middle of a valley. He was tall too - about six feet - and he did not know his own strength. I saw some of the shoemakers of the village urging him to catch Siencyn of Buarth y Capel's old pony and throw him into the ditch, so that he could have the pleasure of pulling the pony out again. Tom got him out somehow but both of them nearly drowned in the mud and water in the Wern ditch. He received two quarts of beer for this feat from Dafydd of Carmarthen and Jacob the shoemaker. Everyone saw how happy Tom's brother, Will, looked that evening after Tom had performed this heroic deed, even though peat and clay from the ditch covered him for his pains.

At this same Cymorth a grand dinner had been prepared which was to be eaten out in the field on a carpet of grass. Great preparations had been made and many delicacies were served. Tom the blacksmith had a ravenous hunger that took some satisfying. Several mischievous lads were prepared to forfeit their dinner if it meant getting Tom to eat their share. Many kept a close watch on him; some went as far as laying bets that he would not eat eight dinners. Even while they talked and took bets, the delicacies were rapidly vanishing. Tom began to look uncomfortable, his face reddening, his eyes bulging and his breathing becoming laboured. But Tom was not beaten yet. Tommy the potter had his eye on him, but said nothing. It was useless asking his opinion of how Tom was coping with his huge meal. He would give it in his own good time. And when he did, he had a wealth of stories, often peppered with terse comments. All he managed to say on this occasion was: 'Only two men in this parish can eat anything like a dinner, Lewis of the Fforest and Tom the blacksmith, and if Tom wants a dinner again today, I dare anyone to tell me what his stomach is made of, the greedy, gluttonous pig! Roll him over or he'll surely burst.'

Most of that afternoon was spent rolling him over and over! Doubtless he said, like someone else from a neighbouring parish who had a huge appetite even after a heavy dinner, 'Oh! for another little roll!' However Tom ate many a dinner after this! If only Tom's mind had been as sound as his body, he would have been an intellectual giant. But as often happens, Nature had been too kind to him physically at the expense of his brain, which was weaker than the average person's. Everybody liked him and in his own way he was friendly enough and pleased to do a good turn for a neighbour. He was one of the simple-minded of the parish and when he put a foot wrong in some way, people such as the mischievous cobblers or others were always ready to make the most of it.

He now lies these many years with the majority in the shelter of Gwynno's church. When we next see him his body and mind will be without blemish; his huge body will contain a strong, able brain, and there, no doubt we will see Tom the blacksmith arm in arm with the angels. He and his brother, Will, spent their lives in the village of Ynysybwl, rarely straying far from its smoke, both living to a ripe old age. The minds of both brothers ran along simple lines. Will was the parish blacksmith and must have shod a great number of horses in his time. He was always at the anvil, yet his earnings were small, barely enough to earn him a livelihood. The old smithy, the anvil and the hammer were all part of him. He desired no better palace than a smithy, no greater happiness than to sit on the anvil or walk around the house, alongside the river or in the garden without having much work to do. He was very fond of simple, amusing stories, many of which he prepared to share with his friend, Tommy Penrhiw, who came along to shoe his mare. Hearing the jokes of these two old cronies was a source of amusement to others in the smithy. Both now lie in the cemetery of Gwynno. Never have there been two more innocent souls, two with less enmity towards their fellows, nor two with less love for hard work!

Will's whole life was spent in one place- Ynysybwl smithy. Towards the end of his life arrangements were made for him to transfer to the smithy at Cwm Clydach to take things at a more leisurely pace and be company for the old couple, Morgan and Rachel Jones. He went to bed one night, thinking to rise early the next morning and collect his belongings, ready to leave the place of his youth, middle age and old age. However by the morning his spirit had left him, leaving his tall, thin corpse behind, to be taken, not to Cwm Clydach but to the resting place of his fathers and a quiet sleep in the churchyard of Gwynno. Thus lived and died William Morgan the smith in the little smithy of Ynysybwl.

'The hammer, the anvil, the smithy he left behind at the bottom of the valley,
Where he lived long and quietly, albeit a life too sparse
As happy as a king was he to wear the leather apron
Whose grain was somewhat tarnished by years of soot and ashes.'

Many years ago it was a common practice to go to the mill to 'thresh' or 'clean' the oats. Little, if any, is done now. The oats of the various farms were brought in turn to the mill to be 'baked'. Many loads of oats were brought to the kiln at Mynachdy Mill to be baked. When the oats had been turned over and over until sufficiently baked, the time came to clean and purify. The oats were taken from the kiln to the mill. There they were put on the 'pin', the water was turned on to the wheel and the husk removed. Some would use canvas sheets to cause a draught; through the two open doors one would fill a skin-sieve of oats as they came through the mill and place it in the hands of Evan Phylip. He in turn threw the oats in the path of the winnowers; in this way the husk was blown away and the pure grains fell into a heap on the floor, soon to be ready for grinding into oatmeal. A mound of husks was always to be seen near the mill and on the other side of the stream was a field called Singrug or Eisengrug, the name no doubt coming from the custom of 'Rubbing the Oats', when the husks were thrown from the mill into the field.

Many remember Evan Phylip. He was a spruce, ruddy-faced little man with a lively walk and always neat in appearance. His feet barely seemed to touch the ground but woe betide any man who came into the mill with dirty shoes! He would beat a retreat more quickly than the way he came in. He was always careful of his appearance whether it was in the house, the kiln or the mill. He was, as they say in Llanwynno, 'as clean as a pin in paper.' We had a lot of fun watching him looking at the feet of 'a lump of a boy' from the country and telling him in a harsh, aggressive voice, 'Your boots are very clean, aren't they?' Then lowering his voice, and speaking slowly, 'Go and wipe your shoes in that grass over there and be careful how you do it, you lout, do you hear me?'

He was notoriously short-tempered. He would quickly flare up

33

like a flame and you would think by looking at him and hearing his strong, quivering, rather sharp voice, that he was a very quarrelsome man. Actually he was a good, just, honest and good-natured man, and although he had a quick temper and appeared aggressive at times, everyone who knew him well realised that beneath the exterior roughness lay a fine nature and a deep tenderness. He was 'King of the Mill' on the banks of the Ffrwd for many years; there I would see him and, in my memory, he and the mill were inseparable. He was fond of his pipe, yarns, old songs and verses.

Like the rest of the Phylip family, he also possessed a sweet, melodious singing voice, which was well known in the locality. I know of no family who for generations were better known for the quality and timbre of their voices than they. Such was Evan Phylip of the Mill. I often heard him singing with a tear on his cheeks and a song on his lips at the same time, while the softness of his voice and the tenderness of his expression were really beautiful. His natural, melodious notes fell upon the soul like the gentle dew of a summer evening. But we must bid goodbye to Evan; his long day is over, though it is sweet to write about him. The mill-wheel still turns and the Ffrwd leaps from Pwll y Crochan (Pool of the Cauldron) over the little mill waterfall as it always did, murmuring softly on a fair day but frothing fiercely when in sudden flood. Now Evan's voice is muted and his chair empty. No flood or storm, no fair summer day, no turn of the big mill-wheel will ever bring his voice back to the kiln and the mill.

Oh! sweet breezes of Gwyngul and Twyn Bryn Bychan (the Summit of the Little Hill), you wander over sacred graves. Forever you whisper above the resting place of many who deserve to be remembered. You play around the earthen pillow of many a quaint old character. Good night, Evan Phylip, good night! May you and Mari sleep the sleep of the just, and when you rise, your new status will be higher than 'the kiln, the harp, the mill and the field.'

CHAPTER SIX

AROUND THE FFRWD RIVER

I don't know how the busy little river that flows from Mynydd Gwyngul down to Ynysybwl to lose itself in the Clydach River came to be called by such a mundane name as Ffrwd (stream or river), but there it is. Ffrwd is its proper name, as Clydach is the name of the other and Taff the river on the east side of the parish. It must have had some peculiarity for the old people to name it Ffrwd as distinct from other rivers.

The other tributaries of the Taff from the mountain and the streams Cynin, Nant y Nawer, Nant Ty'n Wern and Nant Mynachdy were evidently not considered worthy of the name Ffrwd. It is a river noted for its coldness, having a much lower temperature than the Clydach. This is easily explained. Its journey from its source in Mynydd Gwyngul to join up with the Clydach is short. It has no time to absorb the sun's rays as it travels through its narrow banks to the valley. Its bed is also shaded by trees nearly the whole way and springs of cold water run into it on its short journey. Its birthplace is in cold, peaty soil, full of deep and dangerous holes, which would prove hazardous for anyone wandering at night. Indeed, I have often been afraid there when crossing the mountain. These treacherous holes and the peat swamps, whose depth no one knows, make the source of the Ffrwd a place to avoid on a foggy day or a moonless night.

There is one notorious hole that swallowed up a donkey loaded with firewood without leaving a trace. The donkeys were bringing wood over the mountain and one of them wandered off the road a little way, seeking some juicy grass when he suddenly vanished, never to be seen again. John, the carrier, was telling the story with tears running down his cheeks of how the donkey had wandered off, and he the best of the bunch too, and how the little creature went to eternity in a second. No doubt if we could dig down through the peat we would find the donkey and his load well-preserved, as there is little risk of anything rotting quickly in peat. In years to come perhaps some famous geologist will make a great discovery and bring to light a fine fossil of the little creature that went to its eternal rest at the source of the Ffrwd.

Near this spot also there is a spring containing water of the same splendid taste as that of the spa town of Llanwrtyd Wells. Years ago many came to take the waters, but it has been much neglected in recent times. When I last saw it, it was almost lost among the grass, rushes and peatland. One old lady once drank twenty four glasses of the water; why, I don't know, unless it was on the principle of 'kill or cure'. However the old lady proved it was quite harmless as she came there quite often afterwards to drink the same amount.

'Thank God for the water,' she said. 'Yes' said somebody else, 'and for plenty more to come of the same!'

Near the well, towards the source of the Ffrwd, stands a little farmhouse called Rhyd-y-Gwreiddyn (Ford of the Root). It is a hump-backed house, as if it had met with an accident ages ago and had broken its back under the load of thatch. I dare not guess how many layers of thatch rested on the joists of Rhyd-y-Gwreiddyn. I once heard Mr Morgan Jones of Rhiw-yr-Ychen say that it was here that the first public service was held when Nonconformity came to the district. Learning, morals and religion were at a low ebb at that time. It is said that when they had a discussion in the Seiat (Fellowship Meeting) one night on the text from Saint Paul 'Run the race that is set before you,' they all decided to run round the moor at Rhyd-y-Gwreiddyn in order to earn the right to a better and more perfect life! Morgan Jones was over 80 years old when he told me this and I think that he had heard it from his grandfather who had attended the Seiat. To quote him further, 'and they ran and ran themselves to a standstill.' Religion was in its infancy then in Llanwynno, but it soon flourished and many devout and resolute people grew up in the district.

It is worth following the Ffrwd along its journey down to its mouth. It comes from the mountain to the foot of Melin-y-cwrt (Mill by the Court), down to Cwm Downs, then through a strange and narrow cutting, a lonely spot with the wildness of nature still about it. It runs along the banks of Mynachdy Fields and the wooded slope of Fanheulog, throwing it in shadow, keeping it in its dark clutches to work its way through brambles, thorns and undergrowth, frothing noisily in a whirlpool here and there, losing its temper as it rounds a big stone or in a headlong rush dashes down with a splash into a hollow, then hiding under the banks and off through the old 'Golchfa' (where sheep were washed), bursting into song under the branches of the oaks, restraining itself a little as it nears the bottom of Craig-y-Rickets, past Arthur's Wooden Bridge, taking on a solemn note under the rock of the Clwyd Drom, while the big ivy-laden tree shakes its threatening arms over the water.

When it is in flood, the Ffrwd rages against the old rock and the Geubren (hollow tree) which for many years has stood under the ridge. It then passes Ffynnon Illtyd (Illtyd's well), through Golchfa, Buarth y Capel and Cwmfelin, straight on to Pwll y Crochan, where it boils furiously under one of the largest rocks in the country. Leaving Pwll y Crochan and Llun Troed Arthur (imprint of Arthur's foot), it releases a little water to turn the wheel, then leaps wildly like a madman over the rock down to the Mill Pool. Resentfully it then travels past the Bottom Garden and the Smithy Garden, its temper becoming frayed again in front of Aberffrwd, until suddenly and finally it is engulfed in one great gulp by the Clydach, bringing its stormy career to a climax.

Such is the turbulent voyage of many a pilgrim from beginning to end; as soon as he escapes from the mountain pools, he is in the darkness of Cwm Downs or fast by the hollow river bank and on from pool to pool, from one hazard to another, until at the confluence, the struggle ceases. Many of us can see little hope of peace and comfort until life's turmoil comes to an end at the estuary when time means nothing and life has run its course.

'When life's evening approaches and my sun begins to set.'

Since we have reached the mouth of the Ffrwd it would perhaps be useful to descend a little. On the left bank of the Clydach is Cae Bach y Fedw, forming with the other meadows the boundaries of Tŷ Draw or Gilfach Glyd. Many remember the old Tŷ Draw (house over there) whose roof and walls were whitewashed from top to bottom every year, looking like snow. The place was bought by the late Mr D. Edwards who built a grand new house on the site, the old Tŷ Draw giving way to the newly named Gilfach Glyd. (*This is the David Edwards whose framed photograph hangs in the Old Village*

School. It was presented in 1946 by his grandson, Judge Kirkhouse Jenkins, KC, Bath. David Edwards was born in 1801 and died in 1885.)

The house and land were transformed under the robust administration of the new owner. Trees were planted in the rough and unproductive areas, on the grey mounds and on the river banks which had long been barren. Today the farm is covered with beautiful trees. Little or none of the old farm is to be seen, apart from the old barn; it stands where it has always been, by the side of Talar Gwyn (white headland), along the road called Heol Ifan Hywel. It is roofed with grey stones. In spite of all the changes, it looks as Welsh as ever, as if in protest against the innovations that surround it.

Tŷ Draw Meadow is no more. It was a meadow noted for its 'short grass'. It was once wet, peaty, its grass sour and short. But after being drained and manured, it became lush meadow-land. Mr Edwards brought about many improvements in his time. He changed the rough land into productive farm land with a look of paradise to it. Maes y Gaer (the Field of the Fort) still stands unchanged. No doubt it was understandable to keep the old 'camp' or 'fort' as it was. Many a bitter battle has been fought on it, for it was a strategic spot for an army. Here the Welsh upland army camped when the Normans came up the Taff valley. Here the foreign invaders were defeated as they were later on in the parish of Gelligaer, gaining little foothold except in the Vale of Glamorgan. When they came to the hills they found 'the men on the mountain ponies' too tough and swift for them to subdue. Owain Glyndwr and a section of his army also camped at Maes y Gaer, where he was opposed by some Glamorgan men. The graves of those killed are still to be seen and cover the open fields of Tyle'r Fedw. If I am permitted, I shall have them opened soon. Further research is needed on Maes y Gaer.

The road running from Ynysybwl towards Mountain Ash over the top of Maes y Gaer is called Heol Ifan Hywel, after one of my ancestors, one of the Howells of Cwm Cynon, and a descendant of the two brother-monks I mentioned earlier. In the days of Ifan Hywel the first *parish* road was constructed from Ynysybwl to Pentwyn and it was completed under his supervision. Although he has been dead many years now, his name still survives in connection with this road. It has given him a sort of immortality. For my part, it is as worthy as a monument in marble and possibly better and more permanent because of its usefulness. His name has been carved on the road that tradition and the local tongue keep alive from age to age.

But it is time to return to the Clydach and leave Gilfach Glyd with a word to commemorate its late owner. Mr Edwards was a strong, able and sensible man, who lived perhaps a little before his time, as far as the country was concerned. He did much good and the appearance of Tŷ Draw today stands as testimony to his ability as an agricultural reformer and his brave and relentless determination against obstacles. Physically he was a big man. When he was troubled in spirit a great dark cloud rested on his brows and you could see this cloud moving darkly across his face. I never saw anyone whose expression was so changeable. When in a cheerful mood, his face brightened and beamed like the gentle rays of the sun. Life and tenderness shone from his eyes and geniality in place of dark clouds rested upon his large, thoughtful brows. He could tell a good story and had a hearty laugh. His laughter rolled like a great wave with resounding echoes, while nobody enjoyed the noise he made more than himself. He was as strong as Samson but as gentle as a young girl. When roused he became agitated and angry, but his hot passion would subside like an April shower.

These wild swings of temperament showed his strength of personality and the intensity of his feelings. A good poem, an interesting anecdote, an emotional hymn or a quirk of conscience would soften his heart at once and a flood of tears would fill his great, penetrating eyes. In spite of his changing moods at times, I knew of no one with a warmer heart or more love for his country than he. He was inclined to be tactless in speech, which led many to think that he was a perverse and overbearing man, but this was not so. He hated hypocrisy and did not hesitate to speak his mind candidly, whether to king or beggar. He was a great reader and a diligent student with a wide knowledge of things and a memory as rich as a treasure-house. He was a learned, patriotic and a thorough Welshman. He loved his native tongue, he loved the muse, and almost worshipped the land of his fathers. Sadly, he is no longer with us!

Traces of his personality are still to be seen round Gilfach Glyd, but 'his place knows him no more.' No doubt he has left many good compositions during the time he spent with his bosom friend, the poet Alaw Goch. Tŷ Draw is empty without him. I am sad to think that he has been taken from his armchair to the secluded bed in the upland of Gwynno. What shall I do? Cry on his grave? Would it achieve anything to weep bitterly over his burial-place? No! This is a place of slumber. Go quietly and respectfully to the edge of the grave. Place flowers there to brighten the gloom of the churchyard, to cheer the melancholy of the old yew trees, to talk, as flowers talk, of 'better days', for a new dawn to break, a cloudless summer morn, for a more noble and heavenly heritage than the one he left behind, for a softer climate than that of his dear home, and for a life in light eternal, free from all corruption. Farewell, David Edwards; there is no need to add 'Esquire' to his name. Good-bye. May undisturbed sleep dispel his weariness and may he rise refreshed to greet the morning when

'The entrance to all graves will open at the word of command.'

CHAPTER SEVEN

HUNTING

Hunting the squirrel was a pastime for many in the parish years ago, especially on Christmas Day. I remember the first time I took part in a squirrel hunt as a little boy. At five in the morning we all went to service in the old chapel, for it was Christmas morning and I read a chapter to open devotions. The chapel had been decorated with candles of many colours, and they had been trimmed very tastefully by the ladies. A row of candles had been placed round the 'big seat' and most of the other seats and they all looked very attractive. Daniel of Rhyd-y-Gwreiddyn, Shadrach of Llechwen and Williams of Llwynperdid had made a kind of chandelier out of clay from Fanheulog well and suspended it with a long chain from the middle of the ceiling. It was a lovely sight, a good piece of craftsmanship and attracted great attraction. The old chapel looked aglow in the light of the candles. It was now time to start the service. A hymn was announced by Joseph Davies- 'Wele cawsom y Meseia' (Behold the Messiah comes'). Then I recited the chapter my mother had taught me, after which George Davies read out another hymn - *'Three pregnant ladies who were true to their word, Purpose, Promise and the Virgin Mary.'*

The singing was quite spirited. Then Richard Williams got up to break off the end of one of the candles that was burning too fiercely. Everyone watched, afraid that something would happen to upset the beautiful frills round it. Somehow Richard was quite clumsy in his efforts to do what had to be done, for suddenly the decorations burst into flame, forming a kind of bonfire close to the old cupboard. In a second, Mari Tynewydd's decorated candle had burnt out and the smell of burnt paper floated round the chapel. Mari and Richard's daughter, Ann, cast some nasty looks in the direction of the old man who had extinguished the candle before its time. After George Davies had prayed, Siencyn of Buarth y Capel announced a hymn in his own inimitable rustic way. The hymn was *'If in life you serve God, grace and salvation are yours, and while the lamp continues to burn, the greatest sinner grace may earn.'*

Everyone was thinking that if the lamp burnt out as quickly as Mari Tynewydd's candle, some people's chances of grace would be slender! There were smiles everywhere while Siencyn offered a short prayer, during which he said that 'a live dog was better than a dead lion.' This phrase was always included in Siencyn's prayers and he also gave thanks for religion, 'because, but for religion I should have battered my body and bones to smithereens long ago.' Then he concluded, always ending with a great 'Omen', because he was incapable of saying 'Amen.'

Out we went from the early morning service. I heard some of the boys and young men arranging to meet after breakfast to go hunting squirrels in the woods of Tyle'r Fedw and Coedcae Siasper. I decided to go squirrel-hunting with them for the first time. Off we went and by the time we reached the huge oak-tree above the Pandy (fulling mill), there was quite a crowd in attendance; children, lusty lads, young men and even some old men. I was with William of the

Rhiw, Dafydd of Cribinddu, John Morgan of the Lan Farm, Daniel of Rhyd-y-gwreiddyn, Rhys of the Llechwen and the dog, Coryn. We were joined by Siams (James) of Llwynmelyn and his bitch, Fury. Morgan Rhys was there too with the dog, Ship from Tyle'r Fedw. On top of the Darren above the Pandy we suddenly heard a shout, 'Oh! Look, there's a squirrel!'

In a second there was great excitement. They shouted and ran to the trunks of the oak trees, throwing stones and bits of wood at the squirrel in the branches while it jumped from branch to branch and from tree to tree with great dexterity. Off we went through the trees and over ridges; the creature leapt among the branches, making our hearts leap with it. Then we had some bad luck, Siams Llwynmelyn striking his foot against a stone and falling down. He was none the worse for it but he gave cause for mutters of criticism from Dafydd Cribinddu and expressions of annoyance from Siams before we caught the first squirrel. But all this was soon forgotten.

The squirrel had climbed to the topmost branch of the tallest oak in the wood and, while it remained there, there was no moving it. It was decided to send Daniel Thomas up to catch it with a stick attached to a cord. Daniel climbed the tree until he was almost within reach of the squirrel, and then tried to catch it with the looped cord, but not wishing to be strangled in this manner, the creature took another leap, hoping to reach another tree on the other side of the fence and thus evade his enemies. Perhaps due to its being tired, or missing its footing, it failed and came down. But the question was, where? It was seen hurtling through the branches, landing right in the middle of the men and dogs. Where was it? No trace of it could be seen anywhere. Questions were being asked by everyone.

'Who saw it last?' and 'Where did it get to?' Finally Siams Llwynmelyn said,

'I'll tell you where it is. It's in the belly of the dog Ship from Tyle'r Fedw. He must have swallowed it whole.'

And that's what happened, I suppose. The old dog had its mouth open when the squirrel fell, and it vanished like a stone into a lake. There was much more hunting before the end of the day, and the only fracas throughout the hunt was a mild argument between Siams and Rhys the Llechwen, because Rhys doubted Siams' account of the swallowing of the squirrel. William the Clotch had a good hiding from his grandmother for falling over the wooden bridge into the river, and I rather think I had one too for going off on the hunt. Several, indeed most of those who took part in that hunt, have finished with earthly things and now rest in the depth of the grave.

The events of another Christmas Day live in my memory too. We had looked forward with great anticipation to this day, because an important race was to be held between one of the Llanwynno boys and a boy from Mountain Ash. The race was to take place on Cefn-yr-Erw. It was the one topic throughout the parish among men, women and children. Bets were taken for several pounds per side; people were prepared to risk much for the one they fancied to be the most fleet-footed. They knew little about the Mountain Ash man, but you had to support your own parish and cheer on your man as much as possible.

At last the day came. I remember clearly seeing great crowds of people walking to Cefn-yr-Erw on the way to the Cwm. Old men and women were there too, full of excitement - Morgan from the Cwm, Siôn Bach, Ty'n y Gelli and others. It was time to begin, but money had to be 'laid' on the outcome. Where was Thomas Meyrick? Hasn't he come yet? He was the official bookmaker for the boys of Llanwynno. Ah! Here he comes, all of a sweat and asking,

'Who will lend me money? My wife has refused to give me any.'

She was afraid he would lose it all. However he managed to obtain enough for the wagers. Now the course was marked out and cleared. A draw was made for choice of which side to run while Thomas Morgan and Thomas Meyrick were holding the handkerchief at the finishing point. Siôn Jones was in charge of the start. Off they go with a great shout of support.

'They're off! Come on, Llanwynno!'

'Good old Mount! Mount are leading!'

'Now, Will bach, off you go! Oh! Good boy, he's passed the Mount! Go on!'

They are now half-way with Llanwynno leading, and the runner waves to his friends, as a sign that he is bound to win. The shouting now was tremendous as the Llanwynno boy reached the winning post first. Thomas Meyrick was on top of the bank, yelling and throwing his hat in the air. Old Morgan and Siôn Ty'n y Gelli were boasting how much money they had won. There was much uproar and merriment. Before the end of the day, the runner had also won a rifle for shooting at a target that was put up near Ynysybwl. That rifle is now in my possession. I am sure my old friends now scattered all over the world will remember that race and the target if they should ever read this account of that Christmas Day in Llanwynno. There is no harm in recalling these old incidents, although they may appear today to be childish. But 'it is sweet to recall the past.'

I trust that I may be excused for relating the story of a hunt that took place in the parish when I was very young. However I was still old enough to be interested in fox-hunting. The night before the hunt, Siôn the Huntsman from Cwmelendeg (near Cilfynydd) would blow his horn and gather up the hounds from all directions. In the morning we would make for Tarren y Foel to seek out the fox. I remember the morning well; it was not very clear, but rather cloudy with little wind. What wind there was appeared to be lurking in the west. However, off we go, heading for the Darren near Gilfachyrhydd, where thousands of foxes had their lairs. In the valley we see the mist rising in columns and the silence is broken by many hooves and the unaccustomed accents of many men who have come to the valley from all quarters. So excited was the chatter that the Clydach below could not be heard even though it was in flood. The fall of water at the mill has whitened the upper side of the forge with foam. Iantws has left the mill and gone ahead up to Tarren y Foel. There goes Tom the blacksmith, already on the top of Talargwyn, with Will, his brother, climbing the slope and hurrying after him. The children of Mynachdy and Buarth y Capel are here and I with them, all heading in the same direction. Oh! who is this coming behind and walking quickly past us? It's Thomas of the Dduallt who never misses a hunt. Oh, there's Siôn Penrhiw coming along with two dogs on a lead in one hand and his hat in the other; if there's a pool of water anywhere Siôn is sure to put his foot in it. There he goes, Splash! Right up to his ankles. On we go and we reach Tŷ Draw. 'Aha!' What's over there? Oh, it's Mr David Edwards cracking a joke at someone's expense. David Edwards was fond of a rhyme. 'What did he say?' asks someone.' Oh! just this:

'The dog with the finest nose and the best men on foot are good old Turner and Siôn Benrhiw, two who set the pace.'

(Ha! Ha!) *'But the wisest of you all are those on horseback:*

before you footmen slow up on your pace, be sure you have eaten!

(Ha! Ha! Ha!) Away we go, some past Tyle'r Fedw, some towards Gilfachyrhydd Hill, all to meeting on the Darren. What a gathering of huntsmen, and all full of life and eager for the chase. First we have Williams the Lan on his red pony. His great strength is his strong, clear voice, like a silver trumpet, electrifying man, horse and dog. He is now calling on the dogs to pursue the fox. He and Siôn have gone down to the wood below the Darren. Then we see the man from Blaenhenwysg and Ifan Moses, not forgetting Mr Griffith Griffiths too. There, poor chap, is Dafydd Gilfachyrhydd, who revels in the hunt in spite of his lameness. Here's Tommy from the Turnpike. Oh dear! – as usual he falls headlong over a stone, but goes on yelling with the dogs despite his face being buried in the earth.

'Hard to, Turner!' shouts Tommy from the ground.

Here is Rhys from the Llechwen, shouting with Soywal. 'He's out,' he says, 'I'll lay my life on it.'

Down he goes like a boy through the wood, while a crowd of men and boys go as near as they can to the edge of the ridge to look at the hounds. Ifan Richards shouts at us, 'Look out, boys! The fox is sure to make for the gap.'

'Tally-ho!' goes up the cry.

'There he goes, making for Penparc Wood.'

Down they go, men and dogs, after the fox, but Ifan Richards remains on top of the ridge. 'He'll come back in a minute,' he says.

Soon there is a great outcry in the wood; the hounds are baying with one voice, like sweet music echoing from the heart of the old rock, striking the pinnacles of the ridge and flowing down its slopes, while the rousing cries of the hounds and hunters strike a chord of passion. Everybody is on tenterhooks and cannot keep still. The children are yelling and all are frantic- man, horse, dog, yes, nature itself. They seemed overcome and carried away with the heat of the moment. A score of men in the wood are shouting,

'Great! Here he comes! Shush! You on the top, keep quiet! Then Ifan Richard yells,

'There he goes.' Tommy the Turnpike falls down again but goes on shouting.

'There's the fox, on top of the Darren,' his long tail streaming out in the wind. Oh! What a sight he is! He crosses the ridge as fleet-footed as the breeze itself. He looks bold and majestic. The baying of the hounds, the 'Tally-ho!' of the huntsmen, the galloping of the horses has no effect on him at all. He believes he can outwit all his pursuers and get a goose for dinner before midnight. Down we go through the Gelli Wood, over the Clydach, up through Darren y Garth and through Cwm Hendre Rhys. The fox is still well ahead with the hounds keen on the scent. Out comes the old squire who feels his blood warming and his energy refreshed. His shout is joined to theirs. We, who are on foot, are a long way behind, although we have made short cuts over hedges and ditches. We see them now, crossing to the mountain and approaching Llwynperdid. Williams the Lan is in the lead, but he is not tempted to raise the whip to his horse like many others and now he is in Brynmawr field. Yes, there's his voice, his musical 'Go for it!' so familiar to me. Where is Siôn Penrhiw? Oh, he has kept up with the dogs and is nearer than many on horse back; close to him is John Llety Turner. We marvel at the speed made by these two over hill and dale in their excitement.

'I remember the time,' said someone near me, 'when I would

have been up there in front too.' It was Will Rosser, complaining of his asthma, or something that prevented him from walking as well as he used to, but he still hoped to be among the first at the kill. Will was a stickler. He was also very laid-back at everything except the hunt. When he failed to keep up with the hounds and the fox, you could be certain that it was rheumatism, or something similar, that hampered his movements. But on we go, over the Hafod fields to Llwyncelyn Hill, and a voice near me saying, 'We are heading for Tarren y Dimpath.' The man behind the voice was Lodwig, and he knew the ways of foxes inside out. We are now near Hafod Fach. Tommy the Turnpike took another tumble here but this was his special way of making headway! On we go towards Nythbrân Wood. All is quiet; men and dogs have made an end to their shouting and the fox is lost. But soon the scent is picked up, and off they go, led by Williams the Lan, through Cymmer Porth, over the hill, over Craig y Ddinas and out of my sight and hearing. I was so tired I could not go a step further, but Rhys from the Hafod came to the rescue with the words, 'Come and have some bread and cheese with me.'

Two or three of us went back and I can truthfully say that that hunk of bread and cheese was the finest meal I ever ate. I have sat at the table of lords and bishops and dined in beautiful palaces at tables bursting with food since then, but not one of those meals can be compared with Rhys the Hafod's bread and cheese. I was starving, and the starving can eat with gusto.

The fox was caught that evening somewhere down in the Vale of Glamorgan. No doubt many who read this account will be reminded of the things they heard and saw and will testify that this hunt was no figment of my imagination. How many are alive today of those who partook of Rhys Jenkins's bread and cheese? I don't know.

CHAPTER EIGHT

YNYSBWL FAIR

One of the well established events in Llanwynno was the Ynysybwl Fair, which was originally held each year on March 16th. but for many years now the date has been the second Monday in March. It was a celebrated fair, noted chiefly for the animals brought there for sale. It was an early spring fair and, after a long and hard winter, it was timely to hold a fair in a place like Ynysybwl to show and sell the animals. Imagine the scene forty or fifty years ago. We are on the road to Ynysybwl on the morning of March 16th. We are standing by the smithy and the road is thronged with cows and horses. The smithy is closed and William and Thomas are taking the day off, setting off for the fair quite early. But, wait a minute, here's Will coming back, frowning and twisting his legs as though they were whips bought in the fair. He looks solemn and down at the mouth. He is not in the mood for talk and walks to the house. What's the matter? 'Whether it is a fair day or a holiday, there is always work to be done in this place. I've got to change my clothes to shoe the horse from Tŷ-fica.' This little job has upset Will this morning but he won't be long at it.

'How are you today?'

'How are you?' 'What kind of a fair is it?'

'Very slow, so far.'

The speakers are Dafydd Rhys of Llwynperdid and Dafydd from Ynyshir, both of whom have seen many fairs and contributed to the noise there. They remember much of the story of Guto Nythbrân, for their fathers ran about with him on the mountains. Through their parents their memories go back to 1737. They were two thin men, dressed in long grey coats almost reaching to the ground decorated with buttons like five-shilling pieces all the way down. The coats look very heavy, but Dafydd of Ynyshir boasts that he once beat a champion jumper at the Waun Fair with his coat on.

'Turn that cow back, boys! Stop her!' That's the raucous voice of Billy Llysnant, shouting at the cow that wanted to go home. There was no need for her to run, as nobody would buy her. Her horns tell us that she was a calf some fifteen years ago and had been to the fair many times before. Billy looks like the devil in his shiny round hat. The old cow has behaved so badly that Billy has lost his temper. 'What do you want for the cow?' asks Dafydd Ynyshir.

'Anything I can get for the old devil,' answered Billy, and the deal was done - for how much, nobody knows.

At the far end of the field are half a dozen stallions, kicking, neighing and running round till everything is in chaos there. Here we are on the field itself, crowded with animals. Here are the oxen of Mynachdy - 18 of them - sold to Billy Penllwyneinion. There are the small, short-legged oxen from Daearwynno - 14 of them - and all sold. Siencyn Gelliwrgan is holding out for ten shillings more per head for his 18 oxen from the drover.

'Now or never, Jones,' says the drover.

'Never, on those terms,' answers Siencyn.

'Well, split the difference,' says the drover.

'No, I won't; they're going home,' says Siencyn.

'All right, then,' replies the drover, 'get away, you rascal; off home with them; there's no hope of selling them.'

The cattle are turned round and the drover turns to Siencyn offering a rough handshake, saying,

'Well, here's more than they are worth. You are the hardest-headed man in the parish.' 'Yes,' says Siencyn, 'it's no good being soft with a fellow like you.'

A bargain is struck and they are now settling terms over a pint or two of beer. Here we see Siencyn of Buarth y Capel with his old horse, Bowler.

'How old is he, Siencyn?'

'Morgan Tŷdraw knows best,' said Siencyn.

His answer was evasive, for he did not want to lie, and it would be a shame to give the horse's age.

'Whatever his age is, he's quite sound,' went on Siencyn, somewhat affronted by the laughter of some of the lookers-on.

'Yes,' said Lewis from the Forest, 'he would be very cheap to keep, I think. He won't eat much unless he gets a new set of teeth!'

Everyone roars with laughter and Siencyn says,

'Oh, shut up, he's not as old as the chestnut at Gilfachyrhydd, anyway.'

'No,' said Lewis, 'but he'll have a job hearing the cuckoo this year.'

Unable to withstand Lewis's taunts, Siencyn goes off on the old horse. The best cattle are sold by this time. There are some poor ones left and a cow here and there sheltering under the hedge. The crowd now disperses, some to play 'hit my legs,' some to go round the stalls, some to look at Tom Jack, the Berwerdy's, pigs on the river bank, while others go for a drink and to listen to the harp being played. Who is the harpist? Dic Siôn Jones, no doubt.

Siams Llwynmelyn has bought a bob-tailed pig from Tom Jack. This is the pig referred to by Glan Elai ,the hermit, when he wrote: *'Brought all the way from Pembrokeshire just to please Siams Llwynmelyn.'*

Siôn the Tiler pretended to show great concern for the pig, saying, 'Listen, man! A pig without a tail! He won't fatten at all, and a pig must have a tail to swish the flies off.'

Siams, who had a huge chunk of tobacco in his mouth, spat and looked at Siôn, saying, 'Sioni, stop your quips, will you, and leave the pig's tail alone.'

'Stop your talk,' answered Sioni, 'his tail is quiet enough as there's nothing there.'

With a hint of mockery, some of the lads conferred conspiratorially about what could have befallen the tail. One thought he had been born that way, another that the former owner had cut it off as a memento. But Siôn the Tiler was of the opinion that Tom Jack had cut it off and eaten it on the way up from the Neath valley.

'You lazy, childish, uncouth lot,' said Siams.

Off he went in an angry mood. Catherine, his wife, would hear the whole story soon.

Most fun now is to be found in the house. The old hands had gathered in the back parlour, and the noise from here proved that something other than milk was being drunk! Here they are- Lewis the Forest, Siencyn Llwynperdid, the Cobblers and many others. Lewis the Forest was a short fellow, as round as a barrel with a tongue long and bold. He had something bad to say about everyone.

All he wanted was his bellyful of food and drink. No one in the parish had eaten or drunk as much as he. He left his rivals a long way behind. On the day of the fair he would get through two or three dinners, and as for beer, you could not keep tabs on it. His main aim in life was 'Live merrily, and die with a full stomach.' Well, Lewis sits in the corner like a man wrapped in layers of wool, with a set face that looked as if it had been painted red, but he soon proves he is no man of wool, if the drinking of beer and the uttering of barbed comments is anything to go by. Lewis pretends to be very sanctimonious and advises those present to live prudently; all the while, he looks as sober as a saint and brings his sermon to a close by saying:

'Before the sheep depart, the gate to the fold is closed, Discussion precedes Judgment, discretion comes with age; Now is the Day of repentance; Tomorrow may be too late.'

The next speaker is Siôn Bach Ty'n y Gelli, also known as Siôn Patent Cord. He is a very short man but he has the longest arms in the parish and often the longest tongue. He and Siencyn Jones are quarrelling.

'My dear Siôn,' says Siencyn, 'you are good for nothing,' To which Siôn replies, 'I care less for you than for the liver of a louse.'

This led to a fight, and although both were small men, they made more noise and commotion than two giants. Siencyn and Lewis now go out and soon the place is filled with the lads of the village - strong, ruddy-faced boys who bring the fair to an end with general all-out fisticuffs. A stranger would be forgiven for thinking they were murdering one another and that none of them would ever see the fair again. The Hoopers, the Tilers, the Mill boys and lads from other places are all hammering each other fiercely. Night passes, morning comes, and Ynysybwl Fair for that year is a thing of the past, but it has left its mark on many a face in the parish. Next year, exactly the same things will happen again. With one leap, we now return to the present time. All the persons mentioned above are dead these many years, but Ynysybwl Fair still lives, though not as flourishing as it used to be. There is less need for it now, as travelling facilities have brought distant places much nearer to each other.

Another old custom was the Ynysybwl pasty. It was held somewhere about the beginning of August, I think. Janet John Evan would go round the village, inviting everyone to the feast, and at the same time she would earn quite a few pence, for she was given something in every house; a piece of bacon, oatmeal, a chunk of salted beef or even some sheep's wool. Each year it was the custom for an elderly woman, carrying an earthen jug or vessel, to go round, and everything she was given went into the jug. You can imagine what a mixture the jug held at the end of the day. The old lady was called the Lady of the Wool, and I believe she was also known as Granny Mary's Aunt. This same custom was also held in the church of Llanwynno.

Pasties have gone out of fashion and young people know nothing about them, nor of Ann Moses - Nanny Hendre Rhys - who was noted for her pasties in the village and in the church. Nanny and the pasty are now both buried. We note however that a modified version of this custom was held later when all and sundry were invited to a farm or public house where a huge pie had been baked. For a few pence you could eat as much as you liked.

There was a time when the 'Invitation to the Mead' custom was popular in Llanwynno and the mead provided by Jemima of Lower

Clotch House was the most celebrated. A bowl of mead was prepared, with everyone receiving an invitation to the house for the event, usually held on a Saturday night. There was a set of dishes with the dice for the raffle and all looking forward to the night of the 'Mead.' The boys and girls from the surrounding area would come to drink the mead and crack nuts, followed by the eating of apples and round cakes. The boys would take turns to sing some amusing ditties, such as 'The Pig of Tondu', 'The Girl from Penderyn', 'Humphrey the Clog-maker', 'The Little Yellow Guinea' and a host of similar ones.

Then they came to the raffle and there was much speculation as to who would win the tea-set or the silk handkerchief. Yes, they had a lot of harmless fun at Jemima's 'Mead' event. Another attraction was Mari from the Rhiw's home-brewed ale party. Mari used to prepare something stronger than mead for her visitors, and it was only when all the vessels were drained to their last dregs that they left. Edmund would say to the assembled company, 'Now boys, the beer is all gone and the bread has come. It's time to go now before the chapel-goers are about.' Shortly after this speech, the visitors would slip away in various directions, saying in their Llanwynno dialect, 'That was all jolly good fun.'

Any historian recording events that had taken place in Ynysybwl over the past two hundred years would notice that the village was a meeting-place for sportsmen and champions of all kinds. Bando, a famous game throughout Glamorgan, was very popular in Ynysybwl. [*This was a game similar to hockey played between any number up to 15 players per team that was very popular throughout Wales in the nineteenth century; even former Prime Minister Lloyd George is said to have played it! - Author*] It is on record that the men of Ynysybwl had defeated Ystrad and Margam on quite a number of occasions in competitions on the Mynachdy Fields and on the beach near Taibach and other western locations. Cock-fighting was also carried on a great deal at one time and even within living memory this cruel sport had not lost its appeal for people. Pitch-and-toss was also played. The cock-pit and pitch-and-toss areas were clearly marked out when I was a boy with not a blade of grass growing on them. They were located in the fields on the banks of the Clydach, below Tŷdraw, a quiet, secluded, hidden away spot. Today no doubt the railway runs through them and those who pass that way would little think that it was here that the boldest and wildest men of the parish in the last century and the early part of this century pursued these sports.

But Ynysybwl's speciality was the game of hand-ball. The court is still there at the back of the Ynysybwl Inn, where a lot of sweat was lost and a lot of money won. The most prominent players over the past sixty or seventy years were Evan Morris, Evan Phillips, Morgan Thomas (known locally as Morgan Hendre Rhys), Iantws from the Mill and Morgan Blaen-nant; then a little later came Ifan Richard. The last two were doubles-players and they had few equals. Before their time the two Iantws were invincible. The hand-ball tradition of Llanwynno and Aberdare is still the subject of conversation today. The two Iantws represented Llanwynno against Aberdare and won home and away amid the excitement and applause of farmers and iron-workers alike. Later, William Evans of the Graig became champion. I don't think he had an equal for playing 'on the red' as they say. His strength, dexterity with fore-hand either way, his lightness and speed and all-round skill made him a super player and crowds came to see him playing a match.

Often the match ended on a high note with the cry, 'Good old 'Bwl for ever!'

Daniel Thomas was an expert too and was very popular. He had some witty sayings and his actions and speed on the court made him a general favourite. When I was very young I remember him playing left-handed (he was naturally right-handed) against two Ystrad men, named Siencyn the Mason and Ifan Gelligaled. In spite of the handicap he beat them both, much to the amusement of the spectators.

These amusements belong to the past and I don't suppose they will ever rise to their former popularity. They have had their day and were harmless in their way. The young people of Ynysybwl could have taken up worse things. These games developed strength, skill and zeal when there were no other amusements for the young to be had.

In literature too Ynysybwl was quite active. It was in the big room of the Inn that I won my first prize for reciting a part of Cawrdaf's ode entitled, 'A Welshman's longing for his country.' Ieuan ap Iago was the poetry adjudicator, assisted by Ap Myfyr who judged the recitations. The president of the 'eisteddfod' was the late Lewis James of Mountain Ash, brother of the author of the Welsh National Anthem, Evan James. The late Mr Edwards, Gilfach Glyd, was there too. The chief literary awards went to Glan Elai, the hermit, Hezekiah, Ieuan Wyn, and others. The eisteddfod was held during the hay-making, the weather being very hot. I remember being decorated with a ribbon in honour of my first eisteddfod award. The year was either 1859 or 1860.

CHAPTER NINE

THE LAN AND GELLI-LWCH

I am now standing on land belonging to Gellilwch (Dusty Grove) on a cool and breezy day in May. In front, to the east, lie the Cefn and Craig yr Hesg, while the town of Pontypridd nestles at the foot of the hills. Sadly I see nothing but smoke climbing in long columns to the summit of Graig-yr-Hesg, over the top of the Lan hill, to be dispersed there in the purer air of the hills. The chimneys of Pontypridd are much more numerous now. As a result the smoke is thicker. Nevertheless, the air on Graig yr Hesg and the Lan remains clean and free from pollution.

The river Taff has lost its former clarity and flows mournfully through the valley in dark, sombre clothes, traces of coal flecking its surface. The Berw (place of turbulence) of the Taff has ceased to send up white foam and the hammers of the Taff Railway have destroyed more than the beauty of the bridge that crossed the Berw. Oh, all-destroying science! Oh! greedy commerce! How many of Nature's beauty spots are trodden under your feet or swallowed up in your insatiable appetite for wealth, fame or praise! God made the Berw and man made the bridge! Oh, the day of destruction is upon us! But Graig yr Hesg still stands firm. It mocks the railway and the other changes brought by the train. Science cannot pull out her awe-inspiring teeth. Although axes strike at the foot of her beautiful woods, the green mantle begins to creep over her grey ridges and Nature's youth spreads over the bare summit. Meanwhile this high point and the Lan together still throw their shadows over Pontypridd, bestowing their blessing of constant fresh air and water. But now I am right on the very top, higher even than Graig yr Hesg itself.

The Lan and Gellilwch are well-known farms. The Lan stands on top of the hill overlooking Pontypridd. Graig yr Hesg stands on one side of the road leading to Ynysybwl and the Lan on the other. This old residence, Lan Isaf (the lower Lan), looks beautiful on the hill, as white as snow from roof to floor. It is white-washed so often that on a sunny day the place shines like silver to such an extent that the poor old Taff has cause to escape from the valley in shame on account of its filthiness. A few fields further up in the parish stands Gellilwch, built on a rock and shining white in the midst of green fields. Here we have Nature that is undefiled, quiet and undisturbed. Here is the pure air above and the clean earth below, with the hedges, fields and oak and ash trees all donning their spring dresses. Over there we see three or four pheasants in flight towards Graig yr Hesg and wood-pigeons on the wing from the dark wood over the Cadair Ysbryd (devil's chair). Now we see two ravens climbing from the teeth of the hill and croaking above the nests of the jackdaws that live on the craggy ledges. Look! a couple of hares running madly over the Lan moor towards the thick brushwood on the edge of the trees. Let's not disturb them! Shush! Listen to the woodpecker tapping at the bark of an oak tree, on the alert for any movement of insects; and over there is a yellow-hammer and a hedge-sparrow, a stonechat and a redstart perching on the twigs of the hedge, and then off they go in different directions to their nests; the voices of a thrush and a blackbird singing in the nearby copse; the lambs enjoying their young days in the meadow with little thought for the butcher's knife; their minds fixed solely on the rich meadow grass and their mothers' milk!

This is a delectable place! Who would exchange it for the town? If I could, I would put up a tent in this quiet spot, away from the world, and together with my wife and children, would spend the rest of my days in communion with Nature in her utter peace, brightness and sanctity. But there, it is not to be! As long as I am capable of remembering, the picture of these green fields and beautiful woods from the Glôg to the Lan and Graig yr Hesg will ever remain fresh in my memory, yes, until my eyes are closed to the scenes of this world. That may not be long, perhaps. *[In fact, as if he had tempted Providence, Glanffrwd sadly died 18 months later - author]*

The Cefn rises from the Clydach to the slopes of Gellilwch. How charming a place in which to live is this quiet, peaceful Cefn. Mr Davies is its king, living in a stronghold of which he is the owner. I dread to say that there is plenty of coal beneath, and one day, no doubt, it must be extracted from there. When that happens, I hope that the beauty of the countryside will not be despoiled. The spoilers are threatening already, under Glynddwynant. The golden age has passed, and the age of coal is now basking in its glory. What glory! Smoke and ashes and tips as black as Satan!

I mentioned earlier that the Lan and Gellilwch were well-known farms and history connects the Glôg, Penwal, Gellilwch and the Lan with each other. They belong to the same heritage and the same family, named Williams, had lived in them for ages, at least for several generations. Some of them stood as guarantors for others who failed to pay, so the Lan and Gellilwch were sold to cover these debts. Thus the kindness of the Williams' family and the neglect and failings of others caused that family to lose the heritage of their ancestors. However they still remain in various parts of the parish. The owner of the land is Lord Tredegar. Some time later, Richard and John Williams (Richard the Lan and Jaci Gellilwch as they were known locally) sold Graig yr Hesg for several thousand pounds to the industrialist Mr Crawshay, of Iron Works fame. Richard and Jaci owned the farms jointly but they sold out so that each may have his own share. The Crawshay family still own this romantic rock and the land around.

Mr Thomas Williams, who now lives at Gellilwch, is a son of the late John Williams (Jaci Gellilwch) and his wife, Mari. John was the son of John and Margaret Williams, Margaret being the daughter of an interesting figure, the Revd. Thomas Davies, who was known as the Red Vicar of Ystradyfodwg. The reverend gentleman met his death when he and his horse fell over Graig y Ffeirad (the priest's rock) in Ystrad valley. This tragedy occurred on November 17th. 1763. Many people today remember the two brothers, Richard and John Williams as owners of the lease on the Lan and Gellilwch respectively. They arranged matters so that one year the first crop of hay went to Richard and the second crop went to John, the following year roles were reversed. Eventually the lease expired and the land passed into other hands. The present owner is Lord Windsor.

I want to say more about the Red Vicar, whom I mentioned. He acquired the name, 'Red' on account of his ruddy complexion. In his day he was a well-known character. As already mentioned, he perished one night while returning from a journey over the mountain. Due to the fog and darkness he came too near the edge of the cliff and he and his horse plunged to the bottom. He survived the fall long enough to admit that the fault was his, as the horse was minded to go another way. Sadly both went over the precipice to eternity. I have beside me now in his own handwriting the following entry in the parish register: *'Margaret, the daughter of Thomas Davies, Clerk, and Ann his wife, was born on Friday, ye 12th. day of October between one and two of the clock in ye morning, and was baptised on Friday ye 20th day of the same month 1744.'* This girl was the mother of Richard the Lan and John Gellilwch.

One of the Red Vicar's sons, Richard, went to Antigua as a sugar merchant and made a fortune there. His will is now here on my table. He left most of his money to his brothers and sisters, but a great deal was also given to the 'negroes' who worked on his plantations in Antigua. I don't know when he died, but his will is dated 1786, and in it he also bequeathed eighteen shirts to one of his friends.

Another son of the Red Vicar was the Revd. William Davies, Curate of Wootton Bassett, Wiltshire, several of whose letters I have in my possession. Although written over a hundred years ago with the paper now faded and worn, the handwriting is perfectly legible, and what beautiful writing it is! All the children were well brought up and proved to be excellent scholars. The red-faced complexion of the Vicar's family still persists and is to be seen in the fine, gentlemanly face of Mr Williams, the Glôg, while the talent and genius of the Vicar still shows itself in the Gellilwch family, all of whom have a great talent and ability in some form or another.

John Williams died in 1864 at the age of 81. A man of strong constitution, he was a zealous and prosperous farmer for many years. Whatever task he undertook was carried out with thoroughness. He was handsome and courteous, and his grey, eagle-like eyes were clear and penetrating, just like his mind. His strong Roman nose showed the strength and independence of his character. He was well-read and was a thorough Welshman - not like the new-fashioned Welshman but of the good, old type, strong and confident. You could feel authority in his firm, resonant voice and see it in his eyes, his actions and his body language. It would be difficult to find a man more outstanding and skilled in so many things. His neighbourliness and honesty were by-words in the parish. He paid his bills without a quibble, but expected others to be equally fair and prompt.

Near the end of his days he left Gellilwch to live in Pontypridd. Thereafter he spent the last years of his life in peace and tranquillity, enjoying the fruits of his labours through the long years. While his wealth increased he became even gentler by nature. His children lived near him, all in good positions and he had a host of friends around him. As the Taff murmured below his house, passing the beauty spots and richness of the valley on its way to the sea, so the river of his life was nearing the end of its course, passing by the hills of wealth, the rich vales of affection and fellowship, to the river mouth, to the sea, to bring his earthly course to an end. His spirit climbed to the immortal regions from the banks of the Taff, up beyond the summits of Graig yr Hesg and the Lan, past the stars to the spirit-world, but his body was brought to the church of Gwynno, to rest there until the last clear trumpet-call, when he will rise from the shelter of the grave with countless others, and the Saints will be 'taken up in the air to meet their Lord.' There, the history of Llanwynno will end, but, till then, peace to the earthly

remains of John Williams of Gellilwch. May he rest quietly in this
acre of God's kingdom, among the old inhabitants of thousands of
years from Llanwynno. Farewell to him! Many angels come to this
churchyard. The spirit of poetry wanders around the hills here, on
the hill behind the church, on Twyn-bryn bychan and on Dduallt's
fields. It steals around the burial ground; it sings on the host of
graves. Listen to its cry riding on the summer and winter breezes
of Mynydd Gwyngul. Here is a part of its song:

*'You who rest in Gwynno's churchyard, I roam and sing above
you with a host of watching angels here as servants to the host of
heaven. Oh! How many generations are in quiet slumber beneath
the brow? In reply the echo gently murmurs, 'Only He above can
know'.*

*'The waterfall of light sings of nature, songs that echo through
the hollow, while the breezes gently whisper, 'Life anew will come
some day.' To the children quietly sleeping far away from earthly
toil; while the fragrant mountain zephyrs kiss them as they pass
along, Here's a lovely place to slumber after life's weary tasks are
done, here's a lovely place to wake to the call of immortality.'*

CHAPTER TEN

FROM THE TOP OF GRAIGWEN

In case some may think I am concentrating too much on the middle of the parish and inclined to favour one part more than another, I now stand on top of Graigwen. It stands on the Rhondda side of the parish, which here shakes hands with the parish of Llantrisant in the middle of the turgid River Rhondda. Here I am then, in spirit, on Graigwen, in sight of the house of my old friend David Llewellyn, a warm-hearted Welshman. In spirit also I greet him and talk of the times we had in Llwyncelyn and Darrenddu. David was a lover of Nature and what a delectable place Graigwen is for observing Nature dressing up in her spring apparel. This is far better than a doctor's prescription for nursing a man back to health. Oh! Yes! Graigwen is beautiful. Here is a poet's description of it as I remember it: 'Graigwen is steep and wooded with multi-coloured heather, and though her breast is clad in splendour, for scenery her crest is unsurpassable.'

I am now right on top, looking down on the houses situated on the flat ground near the river banks and on the town of Pontypridd. Yes, the Taff and the Rhondda rivers meet a little below the Butcher's Inn. The wild, excitable Rhondda Fawr has swallowed up the Rhondda Fach and presses on indignantly, boasting, foaming and winding its way from pool to pool, until she swoops down into the jaws of the Taff. Her end has come. Her spiralling has stopped. Her wild ferocity has been tamed.

'But the all-conquering Taff soaks up the strength of her tributaries.'

The journey and demise of the Rhondda Fawr is much like the life and death of man. Man starts as a small weakling, then grows and puts on strength; he fumes, boasts and swaggers like the Rhondda in her hollow banks. Look at her charging down the valley. You would think that nothing would halt her progress until she reached the sea at Cardiff. But half-way through her tempestuous career she finds herself in the grip of death, her life suddenly cut short. Yes, such is the end of man's journey after all his passion and agitation, with his great show of life and strength. The end comes suddenly, his voice is stilled and his name forgotten, except perhaps for the gravestone. The Rhondda is absorbed by the Taff, but although death is a fact of life every day, life goes on. As the Rhondda ceases to flow, the Taff will still go on. When the Taff dies a death, the sea still abides like a kind of eternity. Well, that's enough sermonising on the crest of Graigwen.

Now Pontypridd lies below, with the valley stretching delightfully down from the gate of Ynysangharad, past Trefforest, and Rhydfelen, Nantgarw, Tongwynlais to Cardiff itself. The scenery is entrancing. At present I am now living in the Clwyd Valley, the loveliest valley in Wales, *they* say, but, confidentially, I am inclined to doubt *them,* whoever *they* may be. I don't believe there is a more beautiful stretch of scenery to be found in Wales than that to be seen from Graigwen's summit on a fine, clear, summer morning. And I have seen it from every angle. I feel like throwing a challenge to *them* to show me another view equal to it. If the residents of Graigwen were not so accustomed to the scenery, they would be stupefied by its sheer magnificence. But, as the old proverb reminds us, 'Familiarity breeds contempt.' Many times I have stood on the top here viewing the Taff valley in its glory. Truth to tell, I have never seen such a picture of perfect repose and majestic grandeur with the Taff asleep in its bosom and the train making for Pontypridd station with indescribable speed, as if it were sliding on a pavement of ice from the port of Cardiff to the wooded Rhondda valley.

Come with me again, even though you do not see my spirit, and look immediately below us at Pant-y-Graigwen, the Hollybush, and Hopkinstown. The old Rock, with its long escarpment, still looks the same as the time before they worked the coal. But the houses feel the trembling of her knees after the collier or the clay-worker has taken away more than his fair share from the soles of her feet. In her anger she turned and shook the houses and since then it is feared that they will fall to pieces. No one ever imagined that this would happen on Graigwen with its sturdy flanks. There is blame to be put somewhere no doubt and it is a shame that the landowners allow workers to waste their money on building houses that may vanish into chasms out of which the owners have already made a great deal of money. Why don't the people wake up and pull together for the matter to be put right? If they cannot put the heel of Graigwen back as firmly as it once was, they can surely demand justice whereby no chasm or traces of earthquakes would be guaranteed.

Over there is the Hafod [*now known as the community of Trehafod - Author*], the home of the Morgans, true Welsh gentlemen. Morgan is an old Welsh county name, popular and famous in the parish for generations. Welsh is still the language of the Hafod. The whole area of the valley floor from the Great Western Colliery up to Porth is now packed with houses. I can almost remember the time when I could stand on Graigwen and count all the houses and residents, but today it would be easier to count the stars on a frosty night. However the old landmarks still remain. Here we see Graigwen Farm close by, a place that is coupled in my memory with the name of Siôn Llewellyn. Siôn was there when I was a boy and for years later. To me he is part of Graigwen. He was a small man, somewhat comical in manner, always emitting a short, dry cough. An innocent soul, he was very fond of children. He used to question them out of fun in a teasing vein, always stroking their faces upwards, not downwards.

Siôn used to relate amusing yarns to us as he watched the people going home from Pontypridd to the northern parts of the parish. He and Ifan, his son, have finished 'winding the ball of yarn', but they are still remembered with affection in and around Graigwen. Over there we see Rhiwyrychen (Hill of the Oxen), the home of the late Morgan Jones, quite a notable man, a good scholar of the old-fashioned type and unrivalled in history. At about eighty years of age his memory was greater than anyone in the parish. I regret to this day that he died without making a note of the great treasures of his mind. If he did leave any papers, I would be very grateful for permission to examine them some time.

Oh! Yes! Look, there's Hafod Ganol, the old house of George Bassett, and a very important house too. Many still remember the strange old man, George Bassett. The family has a good, ancient lineage going back to William the Conqueror. Many of the Normans married Welsh girls and eventually they and their descendants became thoroughly immersed in the language and customs of Wales. The Bassetts are a large family scattered through the rich land of the Vale and other parts of Glamorgan. George was directly in the Bassett line but no one seems to know how he became such an eccentric and miserly old man. He had a peculiar lifestyle. Certainly he was very well off, according to the standards of the day. He owned the estate whose value was added to at the time of his death by its rich woods. But, strange to relate, the whole lot went 'up in smoke' as they say. Due to litigation and disputes among themselves, the children received nothing and the result was that the old home of their father, George, passed into other hands, to remain there probably.

I knew many of George Bassett's descendants. for whom I have great respect. I would like to see them reinstated in their old home again. The place will always be associated with the name of George Bassett. Cwm George still exists, a community of thatched houses, but still known as Cwm George. The Psalmist is right when he says of mankind: 'Their inward thought is that their houses shall continue for ever and their dwelling places to all generations; they call their lands after their own names. Nevertheless, man, despite his riches, does not endure; he is like the beasts that perish.'

A little further up is the Hafod Fach. One often associates a place with some special person and, to me, when I think of Hafod Fach, the name Rhys Jenkins springs to mind. Rhys was a staunch Welshman and very fond of singing Welsh songs connected with Glamorgan. If I live a little longer I shall put all these songs into one volume, for I too surely am a member of the true Glamorgan breed.

Rhys had the strange habit of singing in his sleep. I have heard him more than once singing a well known ditty from beginning to end while fast asleep in the middle of the night. I heard him one night in his sleep going over all the argument he had had with a man who bought a cow from him at Llantrisant Fair. I was sleeping in the next room and I was able to describe to him the next morning all that happened at the fair, how much money he obtained for the cow and how much he returned to the man 'for luck'. Rhys could be regarded as a good example of the upland farmer: smart in appearance, alert, fond of making money and finding a bargain and then boasting of his skills. Although he was not born in the parish, he spent a good deal of his life in Llanwynno, but when the archangel's trumpet sounds, Rhys will rise from his grave in Llanwynno. A fairly large area of hill area belongs to Hafod Fach. As a result, many of its tenants have no option but to be shepherds.

Penrhiw'r Gwynt also lies on the slope under the lee of the mountain above Porth, within sight of Graigwen. This farm is aptly named Windy Hill as the hill rises steeply from Porth towards Mynydd Gwyngul. Although I think of Billy Rees in connection with this place, he has been dead many years now. He had married a daughter of Daearwynno so making contact between the middle of the parish and Penrhiw'r Gwynt. As children we used to consider Penrhiw'r Gwynt a long way off and dared not think of venturing so far. These old farmhouses have an old-world charm about them. In them you will find the old language and customs of Glamorgan less tarnished by modern living than many other places. I shall be delighted to visit some of them this summer to learn something of their history and make some effort to rescue it from oblivion.

I am sorry to hear that Llwynperdid has been destroyed by fire. A week ago I had described it in a rhyme as 'a sentry in the coldness of the hills'. But even as I wrote, the old place vanished in the flames in its solitariness on the mountain top. How strange! A few days before hearing about the tragedy, I awoke one morning and told my wife about a dream I had had during the night. In my dream I was somewhere in Llanwynno near my birthplace and where I used to play when suddenly the whole place was enveloped in flames. I saw the smoke rising and flames reddening the sky. I thought Fanheulog was on fire and in the light of the flames I could see Rhydygwreiddyn as plainly as if it were there. I woke before the fire was out and the dream caused me much unhappiness. What connection has this with Llwynperdid, one may ask? None whatsoever, I suppose. All I can say is that there was something strange in my seeing a fire in the neighbourhood just before it happened on the hill-farm of Llwynperdid. The old place will rise again like a Phoenix from the ashes to challenge the storms of Mynydd Gwyngul until the Great Fire at the last Day.

CHAPTER ELEVEN

THE CYNON VALLEY

I invite you now to come with me to the hill above Penrhiwceiber farm, overlooking the valley of the Cynon and within sight of Mountain Ash. Here we are near the old farmhouse looking at the old road, the parish road from Llanwynno to Mountain Ash. I am old enough to remember this road in its hey-day, before the 'new road' was made, starting from below Penrhiwcaradog, over Darranlas and down to Mountain Ash. It was a winding road twisting its way between woods, then rushing downhill to the valley, coming out by Clungwyn and then by Nixon's Pit.

This old road still exists and it is very steep. We often wonder how people years ago used to use it at all for so long or how the horses of the parish were able to pull carts up and down such slopes hampered by loads on their backs. Huge, strong oak trees shade the upper half of it, extending their arms in all directions to meet overhead to form a shady avenue. This avenue seems to mask the folly of those who made the road through such high ground. Lower down, on the right, is Cilhaul. What a fitting name this is, 'Sun's Retreat' - much more appropriate than those who named it 'the old *Penrhiwceiber* road.'

There are many opinions about the name Pen-rhiw-ceibr. Some

claim it to be another version of Pen-rhiw-geifr (Top of the Hill of Goats). Of course it is quite possible that goats were driven along the road. However as the name appears on all the old maps for generations, it is difficult to imagine a true Welshman of this parish mistaking 'ceibr' for 'geifr'. Originally the road ran through the centre of a large forest all the way from Mountain Ash to the Lan Uchaf (Upper Lan Farm). In this forest were huge, ancient oak trees, some of them withered with age, holding out their naked arms to meet the breezes that have beaten down on them for centuries, and now looking, in their old age and decay, like the spirits of the Cynon Valley.

The old inhabitants cut their way through these hollow trees to make a road for the ponies that made their way from the Cynon Valley to Ynysybwl. It would have been quite natural for such a road through the forest to be called Rhiw-y-ceibr ('ceibr' meaning 'rafter' as though the avenue of thick trees formed an 'arch'). People of yesteryear often made their roads, like their hedges and ditches, as though their progress was measured from tree to tree. This is why the roads looked so crooked and disorderly, as if they had been constructed by blind men groping in the dark. However I shall refer to the old farmhouse as I have always heard it pronounced, Penrhiwceiber.

I remember the first time I visited the farm. With my hand in my mother's, we went along with Aunt Jemima and William Jones to sample the famous Pasty in the Tafarn Isaf (Lower Tavern), Mountain Ash, and on the way we called at Penrhiwceiber Farm. Dafydd and Gwenni lived there then, although both have long since died. The place shone like amber and the fireplace gleamed like silver. Margaret, the daughter, kissed me, saying that, of the two

Williams I was much the better-looking. 'Ho!' said Auntie, 'If he is the more handsome, my William is the better *man*.' Neither of us was interested in our respective merits for our minds were on better things, the Pasty at Tafarn Isaf.

But let us return now to look at Tŷ'r Arlwydd (the Lord's House), down below, off the road, just before reaching the bottom of the hill. Thomas Charles and Amy lived there and owned the land. It was a freehold farm and public-house. Thomas Charles at one time was well off but his pockets must have been full of holes, for however much money he had, it always vanished quickly. Thomas and Amy were not the money-saving type, it being easier to hold water in a sieve than for either to keep money. A little stream went past the house, and thus was the way of Charles's money. Away it ran at the same speed as it came in, and even in flood, the money went the faster, until in the end, the house, money and land flowed away for good. Some people are like that; they can keep nothing.

Carelessness, neglect and disorder finally brought them to ruin. Thomas Charles was always quiet and irresponsible. Amy was very fond of a cup of tea, sometimes milk or even something stronger. Only the neighbours knew. But Thomas and Amy have now gone to a place where there is no need of a house or farm, and I will say nothing disrespectful about them. If they did any harm, they and the children were the sufferers. Thomas did a lot of good, for he was kindness and friendliness itself. He was a short, sturdy man with a rather comical face; one of those men at whom you were bound to smile. His general appearance and ill-fitting clothes were great cause for merriment to those who met him. His face was somewhat flat and fleshy and his eyes were hard to describe. Each eye looked in a different direction with an entire lack of expression.

All you could see in them was a fondness for a life of ease, with plenty of food and drink, an excess in fact. There was a tendency for him to banter even to the point of crudity, while often chewing a large piece of tobacco - such was Thomas Charles. He wore a short, grey coat, rather ill-fitting, as though made for somebody else. His waistcoat was of red plush material with shining buttons, that was long and heavy but this did not bother him at all. Actually it was big enough to hold one of his children as well, but no matter. To Thomas a waistcoat was a waistcoat even if it could hold half a dozen. His trousers were pulled up too high with the result that they showed a big grey stocking on each leg, leaving space for fresh air to enter above the tops of his Cossack boots. His feet defied description, suffice to say that like those of every eccentric, they were most odd!

Thomas had a thick crop of hair, growing straight upon his crown and well down on his forehead. When I knew him there was no barber to be had in Mountain Ash, so he resorted to using a pocket-knife to cut his hair. He took to shaving every Sunday morning with cold water. Some indeed were of the opinion that the task of shaving was the hardest job Thomas ever did. It was a tremendous undertaking. The shouting and yelling as he dragged at his beard with a razor sharpened on the hob was quite heart-rending. The beard was not so much cut as badly scratched out with the hairs dragged out by the roots causing a mixture of blood, soap and water to flow all over the hearth at Tŷ'r Arlwydd. This was the usual procedure before Thomas considered his face fit to be seen by others, with his chin and side-burns nicely trimmed. It was a pleasant sight seeing Thomas's rosy complexion after its treatment with the razor on the hearth.

News came to Thomas's ears that the railway was to pass through his land and that he would have to sell the land to the company. He was asked how much he wanted for it. 'Oh, the same price as any other piece of ground,' answered Thomas. Word came to Thomas that his land was not as valuable as some other farms - Abercwmboi, for instance. 'Not as good?' was his response, 'it's just as good to provide a railway as any of them!' Some say that this was the cleverest remark Thomas ever made in his life. Anyway, the land was bought, the railway came but the money was of no lasting benefit to Thomas; it slipped through his hands like everything else and in the end Thomas and Amy slipped under the curtain of the grave to rest, far from the noise, the railway and the money and cares of this life.

Tŷ'r Arlwydd still stands near the little stream although great changes have taken place in the district. I believe that Clungwyn is still there. Gwernifor and Darrenlas are no longer farms where cattle graze and lambs gambol. They now form part of the track where the 'fiery steed' [*the railway – author*] weaves its way on commercial errands through the Cynon Valley.

Opposite us, on the other side of the Cynon, is the old house of David John Rees, who, like his father, was fond of singing and playing the flute. Both now lie in the silent land and the old house is a moss-covered ruin, tired of waiting for the day of its release, like its former owners. I remember seeing Rhys of Darrenlas and others cutting hay on the peaty field there on the spot where the Baptist chapel now stands, surrounded by several houses stretching as far as the Taff Vale Railway station.

In passing I must mention a few of the old residents whom I have seen making their way around Mountain Ash. There was Morgan from the Dyffryn, a man who had a good deal to do with the beginnings of Mountain Ash, especially the Caegarw side of the valley. Again there was Edward Thomas, the Hooper, who for years was minding his own business making money in the chipping shed on the banks of the Cynon, within the confines of his own garden. Before him I remember Dafydd from Troedyrhiw Farm, and Gwennie, his wife, often going down to the village before it threatened to become a big town. Where is Siôn Morgan, the tiler? He was a monoglot Welshman, of the best Llanwynno breed, always full of fun and as boyish in spirit at the end of his life as when he left Ynysybwl. He and Jemima are among the majority who, as the book of Job says: 'are glad when they reach the tomb and rejoice when they come to the grave.' Then there are the Darrenlas boys, Rhys and William and the boys of Penybanc. They are all getting older and one by one are falling into the long, deep sleep. Evan Evans from Allen's, Thomas Williams the butcher; dear me, if I had the power of the Resurrection, I would be able to recall a great number from the land of oblivion. But 'sleep on and rest'; the dawn will break.

I have often wondered why Mountain Ash, with such strong Welsh connections, was burdened with an English name. Why don't the inhabitants try to adopt a Welsh name for the place? Here it is, in the heart of the hills, in the valley of the Cynon where Welsh is the language of everyone, with the mountains, the woods and the farms all pure Welsh, and then to be named in English after a native tree. Mountain Ash indeed! Would it not have been lovelier, easier and more natural to have called it 'Y Gerddinen' or 'Y Griafol?' (both of which are Welsh names for the mountain ash tree). The farm Pantygerddinen, a well-known landmark higher up the valley, sounds much more fitting. But it's no good prattling on! The damage has been done and the place will always be known as Mountain Ash. The two farms, Upper and Lower Forest, have long been anglicised but the Maerdy has remained purely Welsh all along. But here I must shake hands and bid you farewell in the shade of the great oak-tree on the old Penrhiwceibr Road. Everything is Welsh here, from the bed of the river up to the twig of the oak and on to the summits of Penrhiwcaradog and Mynydd Gwyngul . In these places you will find Welsh to the end of time!

CHAPTER TWELVE

TROEDRHIWTRWYN AND GUTO NYTH BRÂN

Troedrhiwtrwyn is the name of an old farmhouse at the upper end of Graigwen, not far from the Great Western Colliery in the Rhondda Valley. The place is growing rapidly, but originally consisted of Troedrhiwtrwyn and Typica only. Later Tymawr joined them and gradually the whole area became known as Troedrhiwtrwyn, after the old farmhouse.

The name is apt and descriptive. The road from Pontypridd past the Hafod and the home of George Bassett, Yr Hafod Fach, Nythbrân Farm to Penrhiwgwynt, starts from the valley at this point. The Hafod slopes down here as if it were pushing its nose into the valley and river. The steep hill from Blaenhenwysg to the valley comes to an abrupt end here with the adjacent hill rising from the vicarage behind the Great Western, or Calvert's old pit. As can be seen from the name Penrhiwtrwyn (Top of the Hill like a Nose), the hill with the steep slope ends here. The old farmhouse is now surrounded by houses of a more modern and fashionable kind, but it still remains like a patriarch bowed among its descendants. Although it looks worn out and enfeebled, there is something more majestic and poetical about its appearance than the newer houses, as if it still consorted with the spirit of the past, cocking a snook at modern ideas but identifying with things older, more deep-rooted and more Welsh in character.

What a contrast there is between the names 'Great Western' and 'Toedrhiwtrwyn'. There is nothing poetic, of antiquity, of historical worth or Welsh about the name, 'Great Western' - nothing but all that is anglicised and commercial, but in the name Troedrhiwtrwyn we have depth, vividness and patriotism. The sound takes us back before the days of coal, clay distilleries and things English, to that period when places were named after Nature, as befitted their location and relationship, by the old poets and philosophers of the uplands who never erred in naming a mountain, valley, river or house.

Yes, Troedrhiwtrwyn, that grey old farm resting on the slopes of the Hafod and Blaenhenwysg, is like a pilgrim of the past. I could stay here visualising a thousand images of the old building and its former residents, of the peace that reigned there before traffic on the Rhondda road was but slight, yes, even before there was a Rhondda road at all. Then one heard but the murmuring of the river or its roar in flood or when it swirled furiously in the treacherous pool. The same images throw up visions of strong winds blowing from the direction of Cymmer, sweeping through the Hafod woods and over Graigwen itself, howling a challenge in the teeth of the Cwar Pica (the sharply-outlined quarry). I wonder who lived in this valley in those days of yore? Their names are lost and their graves are gone like the leaves, for ever, until we reach the days of Guto Nythbrân, and later, George Bassett, then William Ready and his amusing contemporaries.

I must avoid letting my imagination run riot. I must apply myself to the few facts that are known about Troedrhiwtrwyn and allow my readers a free rein regarding its past. Some fifty years ago, a fine field of wheat grew on the spot where the vicarage now stands. It was the home of the Reverend Moses Lewis, the present vicar of Llanwynno, an able and talented man. I can say from personal knowledge of him that there was never in Llanwynno a vicar more able, patriotic, warm-hearted or fervent than he.

The aforementioned fine crop of wheat was safely garnered and the barn at Troedrhiwtrwyn was filled with the heavy yellow sheaves. The owner was proud of this good crop. All the troubles of gathering and storing it were over and there was no fear from rain and storm since the barn was like a city of refuge separating owner and foul weather. But as so often happens, 'the more secure we feel, the nearer to disaster we are', and such was the case at Troedrhiwtrwyn. A huge army of rats suddenly invaded the farm, rats as big as cats. The plague was so bad in this part of the Rhondda valley that all the wheat in this barn was either spoiled or destroyed. When the precious sheaves were inspected, they were found to be worthless apart from a few grains which were taken to the farm.

The rats now deserted the barn and took possession of Troedrhiwtrwyn itself, which quickly became the abode of this merciless horde of rodents. Every corner, every cupboard, every wall concealed rats of all descriptions. There was never such a plague since Pharaoh was over-run by frogs. Men, ferrets, cats and dogs were of no avail. The rats increased in number, grew stronger and bolder and regarded themselves as greater than conquerors. They not only took food from the dairy but carried girls' petticoats and children's clothes to their holes in the walls. The residents of Troedrhiwtrwyn knew no peace, comfort or safety. The matter had become a serious one. Either the people or the rats had to go. How were they to get rid of the rats? They treated the cats and dogs with contempt. Then some of the inhabitants heard that if you caught one of the rats and burnt its hair with coke or cinder, the others would take fright and run off. So they decided to catch one.

As Daniel, one of the servants, was going upstairs one day, he caught one very big rat. It was as fat as a porker as a result of eating the good food and living the easy life in the barn, while the hair literally glistened on his body. He had the look of a well-fed stallion. At last though he was caught! He was set on fire, at least red hot cokes were poured over him and he was allowed to run away, enveloped in flames. No one ever thought that a rat could emit such terrible screams. The cry was far more piercing than that of a pig on the butcher's bench when its large neck veins were being cut. Up the steps went the rat like a goblin breathing fire and brimstone only to disappear into the first hole it saw in the wall. What became of it is not known. What is known is that the effect on the other rats was negligible. The plague remained in spite of the burning and his mates grew bolder still.

One night the farmer went to bed rather early, taking with him a loaded shotgun to start war on the rats by shooting them. During the night, hearing the movements of the army of rats in the room, he fired and killed two of them with one shot. The rats took such fright that they fled immediately and were never seen again at Troedrhiwtrwyn. Apparently they rushed headlong into the river Rhondda and swam as fast as they could to the ships at Cardiff. Anyway Troedrhiwtrwyn was at last freed from this strange plague. But even more strangely, when William Thomas fired from his bed into the melee of rats Mari, his wife, asleep at his side, did not even wake up at the sound of the shot. Although the gun made a noise like thunder and the room was filled with smoke, it all went over

Mari's head. She stirred neither hand nor foot, much to the astonishment of her husband, who thereafter often remarked, 'I can't understand how the goblin slept so soundly.' The old man was recently buried at the age of 86, not at Troedrhiwtrwyn but Abercwmboi, near Mountain Ash.

A little higher up on the same hill, a mile or so from Troedrhiwtrwyn stands another old farmhouse, named Nythbrân (rook's nest). There is nothing unusual about the place, which is an old white-washed house with a roof of grey stones, standing several fields up from the river. I wonder why it is called Nythbrân? The answer is not clear. Most likely it is derived from its location, where rooks nested in the nearby trees. Perhaps its name is taken from a person called Brân, who may have lived there. This is of course pure conjecture, without a shred of history to prove it. But I have the history of one man who lived there who has made the place famous to all, even to people living as far away as North Wales. The house is no more distinguished in location or resources than any other farm in the parish, but it has been immortalised because of its association with the fastest runner in the country, perhaps in the world of that day – Guto Nythbrân.

The story of Guto or Gruffydd Morgan is undeniably authentic. I have spoken to old people whose fathers knew him. One in particular was Dafydd Rhys of Llwynperdid, whose father had often run with Guto and helped him when training on Mynydd Gwyngul. Guto was born in Llwyncelyn (Hollybush) in 1700 but his parents moved to Nythbrân when he was very young. He grew up a fleet-footed boy with nobody his rival on the flat, on the steep hillsides or on the wild mountain top. He was so fast he could catch a young sheep whenever he liked. Many have performed acclaimed athletic feats but Guto's achievements could be likened to the days of King David in the Old Testament. Sometimes he would be sent by his mother to Llantrisant for some yeast. It is said that his mother would put the kettle on the fire for breakfast as he was leaving on his errand. He would cross the Rhondda river by the Pyllau Duon (black pools) near Britannia, climb up the side of the mountain in a dead straight line, ignoring road, wall, hedge and ditch, and, although the distance was all of twelve miles, Guto would be back with the yeast before breakfast and the boiling of the kettle.

His mother once sent him to Aberdare on a message while she had some business to attend to, with hopes of a gossip and a pinch of snuff in Hafod Fach. Away he sped over Cefn Gwyngul to Cwmaman, thence to Aberdare with the message. His mother thought it was time to return home to prepare Guto's dinner, only to find he was already back. She would not believe he had been to Aberdare until she was convinced by the message having been successfully undertaken.

There is a story and a tradition that he was once asked by his father to gather up the sheep on the mountain and bring them down to the yard at Nythbrân.

'Go,' said his father, 'and take the dogs with you and bring the sheep down as quickly as you can.' Guto answered, 'Keep the dogs here, I'll do better without them.'

Away he went. He brought the flock into the yard in a very short time, without the aid of man or dog.

'Did you have any trouble with the sheep, Guto?' asked the old man.

'No', said Guto, except with that reddish-grey one over there, but I caught her and broke her leg.'

'Listen, boy,' said the father, 'that's a hare. What on earth are you thinking of?' Where did you find her?' Guto replied,

'She rose from the ferns on Llwyncelyn mountain and before she reached the Hafod, I caught up with her and then she had a nap with the sheep.'

'You are a silly fellow,' said the father.

I heard many of the older people speak of Guto's great courage when he followed the fox with the Llanwynno hounds all the way to a corner of Cardiganshire. It was dusk when the fox, two hounds and Guto had reached a spot near a gentleman's house, with Guto and the hounds too exhausted to catch the fox. Guto was warmly welcomed by the gentleman and later ran several races with the man's horse, which had lost him a lot of money through having come out second best to another gentleman's horse. The result was that Guto ran against this man's horse and beat him, winning back all the money which had been lost and more to boot. Guto returned to the Rhondda valley, where he was applauded only by the strong breezes of Mynydd Gwyngul joining in the song, 'See, the conquering hero comes.'

I can remember some of the old people – many over eighty years of age or in their graves by now – relating with great relish Guto's journeys and races. Although he would complete long journeys in what appear to us to be incredibly short times, these old-timers had not the slightest doubt of their truth. They could recall his preparations for a race. He would sleep on a warm heap of manure in front of the stable, the natural heat of which would loosen his limbs until his muscles were like whip-cord and as flexible as whalebones. Although there were many fast runners to be found on the hills in this pastoral community, there was no one to compare with him on a twelve mile race. He was like one of the deer that

Solomon referred to on the hills of Judea. It is on record, as I mentioned before, when Guto led the hounds to Cardiganshire, that he kept pace with the dogs over hill and dale, through the briars of the lowland and the solitude of the upland, over moor and meadow, often achieving the capture of a fox by its tail.

Siân the Shop was Guto's best friend. She staked a lot of money on his prowess as a runner. It is said that many a rich gentleman in the country today has derived his wealth through her enterprises. Near Troedrhiw-y-cymer there were two small thatched houses which made up the Shop, Siân's home. Her name will always be linked with that of Guto Nythbran. She once made a small fortune when a race was arranged between Guto and an English army captain from Carmarthen who was stationed at Hirwaun with his troops. The course was over four miles and the prize money was five hundred pounds, which Guto won comfortably. Then another challenge came from another Englishman, called Prince, for a contest over a twelve mile course for a huge sum of money.

The challenge was joyfully accepted by Guto and his friends and off they went to Caerffili to arrange the terms and the course. A day was fixed and the runners were to start from Newport and finish near Bedwas church. Hundreds of pounds had been wagered on the race with all the wealthy of the parish placing their bets on the superiority of Guto's speed. Siân the Shop, now regarded as a rich woman, was there, naturally. It was said that she wagered an apron full of sovereigns on Guto's legs. She was always generous where Guto was concerned but this time she risked her all on him. The runners set off and soon left Newport behind with Prince in the lead and drawing further away all the time. Guto lagged behind to stop and chat with some onlookers until Prince was well out of sight.

Then Guto saw it was time to move on, saying, 'I must remember Siân the Shop.'

With that he sped like a hind over the dale. When some of the other man's supporters saw that Guto was gaining, they threw glass on the road to try to cut his feet and cause him to slip, but he leapt over it and ran like a deer. As he was ascending the steep slope towards Bedwas church, Guto overtook Prince and, as he did so, asked him if he couldn't travel a little faster. It appears that Guto ran for a time side by side with Prince, but again remembering Siân and her money, he sped on like a mountain breeze to finish the race in seven minutes under the hour- twelve miles in fifty three minutes.

So overjoyed was Siân that she ran forward and clapped Guto on the back, shouting, 'Guto Nythbrân for ever. Well done, Guto'. In thumping him heartily on the back she had little thought of the hard race he had run and that his heart was beating wildly as a result of the final spurt. His heart jumped out of its place and Guto finished not only a course of twelve miles but his last race on earth! While Siân the Shop was taking her winnings of two aprons full of gold, Guto was closing his eyes on all the trouble and kindness, wealth and poverty of this world, at the age of thirty seven.

The grief that followed in Llanwynno was poignant. The remains of this wonderful man were placed to rest near the south wall of Gwynno's church. On the grave was erected a suitably-inscribed stone on which was carved a heart, indicating the tragic way in which the great runner died. Twenty years ago the people of the parish placed a large tombstone as a fresh memorial on Guto's grave on which are written the following two verses, the work of Meudwy Glan Elai and Glanffrwd.

'He was a nimble and courageous runner, a giant and a winner;
may his name for ever be kept alive and radiant.

This stone was placed by us as a token of affection; may his
ashes e'er remind us of this justly famous man.'

I have not embroidered the story of Guto but rather selected the
most colourful highlights from the maze of tradition.

CHAPTER THIRTEEN

PONTYPRIDD AND SOME NOTABLE CHARACTERS

We are now standing near the Old Bridge over the Taff in the town of Pontypridd and I am in the company of many old friends. We gaze at the magnificent arch rising over the river, looking so solid and grand. The Taff, flowing under it, seems to be swallowed up in the enormous gap. The builder of the bridge, William Edwards, had erected three arches before this one, on the very same site. I believe that he began the work in 1746, but having survived and proved itself as a useful crossing-place for some time and an object of admiration to all, a great storm arose in the Taff valley. The wind blew fiercely, destroying trees in the valley and on the uplands, while the Taff became more turbulent than usual. On the bulging waters huge trees came down and piled up against the supports of the three-arched bridge, forming a tremendous dam across the river. The weight eventually proved too much and the whole structure was swept away in one fell swoop.

Undaunted, William Edwards decided to build another bridge, one judged to be safer and more firm, if at all possible. This time he dispensed with the centre supports, leaving the bridge with one single span, measuring 140 feet by 35 feet. By the year 1751 the new bridge was completed except for the side supports or hand-rails. But again it was a case of disappointment for Edwards, the people of his parish, Eglwysilan (on the eastern side of the river) and those of the adjacent parish of Llanwynno (on the western side). Owing to the enormous weight, the locking-stone collapsed and the whole structure fell into the river. But William Edwards was not that easily defeated. A third attempt was made; this time, in order to lessen the weight, he made three holes on either side of the bridge. This also added to its charm from the aesthetic point of view. This great one-span bridge was finished in 1755, nine years after Edwards' first attempt, and it still stands as a monument to the skill and persistence of the bridge builder from Groeswen.

Up to the year 1830 this was the longest single-span bridge in the world. A later one, built at Chester, was just a shade wider. Crowds came from far and wide, including the Continent, to see the Pontypridd Bridge and to admire the work of the famous self-taught builder from Groeswen. The day of the Old Bridge is done and it now looks down on the New Bridge built underneath it with a royal, patriarchal air. Its main fault was that it was too high, making it difficult for anyone with a heavy load to negotiate both inclines. Here are some verses of Iago Emlyn in praise of Edwards' masterpiece:

'Here is an arch as a covenant, a noble brow above the waters below, a rainbow over which while it stands, never will one see a flood. A span, a hanging heap of clay and stone as portals of the flood, A bow that joins two heavy banks for the stream to flow between; Gyfeillion's meadows are thus linked to the rock of Ifor Lleision, a crested cover on the cauldron of the deep to escape the

threats of the Taff. Here is a stony pile, a steep-rocked bridge,
unassailable columns holding their arch, shaped like the bow of a
yoke; spacious and strong on the mane of the waves, as a jaw it
opens to swallow, like the mighty gorge of an abyss, the river pours
its deluge above Ifor's floor and frowns at the sea from its banks!
While the Taff remains, Oh bridge, stand firm on your foundation
in eternal memory of the man and a monument to his skill.'

Now we are near the old home of Gwilym Morgannwg, a good poet,
an excellent Welshman and a true patriot. Pontypridd has done
nothing to keep his memory alive. Iago Emlyn once paid a visit to
Gwilym Morgannwg and, seeing his beautiful library, wrote the
following verse:

'A retreat of the artist's treasury, a house where the Muse resides,
a delicate gem from the vale of thought, the fire of genius gives
sparkle to the day.'

The reputation of Pontypridd was once celebrated throughout
Wales, not least for its literary activity. Just look at the shining list
of bards and writers associated with the place even in my
experience, and that is quite a short span of time. A native of the
district, if not the town, is Ieuan Ddu, the father of the revival of
Welsh music and editor of the 'Cambrian Minstrel'. He was the
connecting link between Pontypridd and the music and literature of
our nation and also with the important Eisteddfodau held in
Abergavenny, a period of renewed life in our literature. He carried
in his breast the fire from these altars and brought fervour that
ignited the people of Pontypridd. Here also I knew and admired
Ieuan, the son of Iago (Evan James) who has given immortality to
the town by composing 'Hen Wlad Fy Nhadau' ('Land of my

Fathers'), the Welsh National Anthem, - a song that will endure when even Graig yr Hesg will have been dashed into pieces. Then again we have Myfyr Morgannwg, a poet, antiquary and Welsh scholar who is unequalled. He has taken on the mantle of Iolo Morgannwg and is regarded in Pontypridd as a patriarch upon whose shoulders rest the heavy burdens of experience, learning and years. May his life's closing years be peaceful.

Another scholarly bard is Dewi Wyn o Esyllt, whose 'Ceinion Esyllt' will always remain popular and whose admirers will still be undiminished when Welsh literature celebrates its millennium. His knowledge and literary skill are much acclaimed. Then we have Carnelian, whom I consider to be the finest writer of the 'englyn' (Welsh 'four-lined verse') in the country. He has won a houseful of bardic chairs but still keeps a corner ready to accommodate more of them!

Near by, up on the hillside, the bard Brynfab looks down from his home in Eglwysilan. He possesses strong poetic skill, scholarship and a first-class intellect. If there had been no sheep or cattle to be troubled with in the world, he would, like Gwilym Hiraethog, have been one of the nation's leading poets. In spite of all his animals and farming concerns, he has made good progress as he has climbed towards the top of the literary profession. Quite near lives Merfyn, a natural poet, capable of lovely imagery but whose work needs to be more polished. On his mother's side he hails from Llanwynno. His father lived there too for many years, ending his days there in peace. Merfyn learned his poetic craft in the sacred valley of the Clydach. As a boy I was carried to school on his back hundreds of times. I suppose that is how I caught something of the poetic spirit from him! He composed that delightful poem, 'Y Bwthyn yng nghanol y wlad' ('the cottage in the heart of the countryside').

Then there is Moesen, an artistic little poet, full of wit and drollery. Unfortunately his work as an auctioneer, an executor of wills and of making money prevented him from pursuing the Muse that he loved. Nearby is the fluent, amusing and patriotic Morien, a Welshman from head to foot, and one of the liveliest writers of his day. Ap Myfyr again was one of the most skilful poets in the country and was almost unsurpassed in his composing of the 'englyn' metre. His genius had its limitations but he was vivid and passionate. If he did not exactly resemble a mighty river, he was as one of the purest rills in the forest of poetry. It was lack of time that caused him to miss out on winning bardic chairs, not lack of skill. There are many for whom the Muse has been fettered in its bearing of fruit because of enforced circumstances.

Here lives Ieuan Wyn, who, when young, gave promise of gaining a name for himself. However the Muse, after early success, became tired and failed to live up to expectations. If it had not been allowed to wane it would have waxed strongly with the rest. Ieuan Glyn Cothi once lived here and may return one day. He has little time for composing as civil servants are not paid to dream.

Dewi Haran, another lover of the Muse, also lived here for many years. He died two or three years ago, being ever faithful to his country, its Eisteddfod tradition and its literature throughout his life. He and his old friend, Ap Myfyr, lie near each other in Glyntaff cemetery. While the two poets are now muted with their harps hanging on the willows of death, the birds in Eglwysilan still sing in Welsh and the Taff softly whispers as it passes by. Though their voices no longer sing, their songs and poems live on.

Let us make our way up to Mill Street, that narrow thoroughfare that looks as if it is trying to prevent the people of Llanwynno and those from the Rhondda from coming to town except in groups of one and two. It was however wide enough for John Griffiths and Aaron Cule to make their fortunes there. Business still flourishes here with the increased population. We now pass the home of Mathonwy, a man whose gifts are as brilliant as anyone in the town. I have works of his in English and in Welsh, both of which are of high standard. He could have been nearer the seat of the immortals than he is. Nevertheless, he has written many things that will never die. When in the mood he was a zealous patriot and jolly company.

Here we are travelling through Hopkinstown. Why, in Heaven's name, is it not called Tref Hopkin? This is the place where William Howell, the good Ivorite, lives. As we turned off the Graigwen Road below Carmel chapel, I should have mentioned the house of Gwyngull. He was another keen Ivorite and a poet who has now come south, although his poetical skill was nurtured in the big Pond in Anglesey known as Llan-fairpwll-gwyn-gull-llanmathafarn-eithaf-ger-llandysiilio-llandygogo-goch! He is truly one of the bards of Pontypridd.

Passing through Gyfeillon, we are still in the parish of Llanwynno. Gyfeillon is the name of an old village now merged with Hollybush below it and Hafod above it. These landmarks have altered and grown during the last few years. When I began my literary career, the district round the Hollybush and Pant-y-Graigwen was the home of many fine poets. Where is John Davies, for example? And where is Thomas, his brother? They were two gifted poets. The two Morgan Morgans have died and lie side by side in Llanwynno. From Gyfeillon the voice of Rhystyn sings no more. Tawenog still lives and bursts into an occasional lyric. Eos Hafod also is still to be found among the thousands in the Rhondda. Penwyn again, where is he now? Alawfwyn, namely, Richard Evans', voice has ceased to be heard these many years. He laboured so hard in the world of music that his strength finally gave out, not yet having reached the peak of his career. Siôn of Llanharan has given up the office of deacon and, with it, his naps in chapel! The simple-hearted William Rosser is in his grave and the chapel he attended to enjoy the feasts of the Gospel has been destroyed by subsidence or something similar. Another chapel has now been built near the same site. Today, Ynys-yr-Hafod is one mass of houses which, with its regular pattern of streets forms quite an attractive township.

As I passed through the place recently, I felt the desire to call out the names of the old residents. 'Phylip William, answer me!' No one answered. 'Mari Phylip William, where is she?' She is silent for ever. 'Mari Scott, come to the door!' She does not come and 'the place knows her not.' 'Siôn Siencyn!' His worldly burdens have been cast for ever into the lap of the valley. Well, well, the place is quite foreign to me now. Few of my old friends remain and they are approaching the sunset of life. Yes, this part of the Rhondda valley is famous. Cadwgan of the Axe lived here. When Welshmen were needed to defend their country, Cadwgan would travel through the valley, sharpening his battle-axe. 'Cadwgan, sharpen your axe!' became the war-cry of Glamorgan.

Now we are standing by Darren-y-Pistyll (the Waterfall of the Knoll), near the little house where George Bassett died. This strange man had moved from Hafod Ganol to one of the little white houses at the foot of Darren-y-Pistyll where he spent his last years. The waterfall was there in Cadwgan's time. I don't suppose the men of the Rhondda take much delight in the view from here in their early morning rush to work. During the hottest weather, the waterfall dries up quickly. But when the rain falls on the hills, you will see the Pistyll leaping over the ridge, seething and foaming, while occasionally a rainbow envelops the whole scene like a halo. What a glorious sight! When the little river is in flood, leaping from rock to rock through the ravine of Cwm George, its heart seems to gather pace and gain strength as it nears the edge of the fall, then in one great leap it forms a semi-circle of pure, white water. Indeed, so white is the fall of water, that it looks from a distance like the brilliant, shining hair of the angels of the hills, hanging loosely over the ledge. This serves as the only remnant with the past and we are grateful for it. The collieries have changed the whole outlook of the valley. The present scene offers the beholder the Hafod and Coedcae pits, which appear like sins that have degraded the Garden of Eden and covered everything with blackness. But, in time of rain, the Pistyll remains today as it was at the beginning of time. It rushes along as it always has and roars as it did centuries ago! It foams, it leaps, it scintillates, still retaining its distinctive Welsh quality and its turbulence as it did long before the Norman invader ever set foot on our soil.

CHAPTER FOURTEEN

CWM CLYDACH AND SIÂN PHYLIP

If you were taking a walk from Aberdare through Mountain Ash towards Ynysybwl or Llanwynno, you would have to make your way slowly up the new Ceiber Hill road, leaving Darranlas on your left and proceeding under the shadow of Penrhiw Caradog ridge until you reached the top of the Lan. From this spot you can look down on the Cynon valley and see Mountain Ash on the flat land below, rising on both sides of the valley like a bird spreading its wings for flight. Moving on from here and crossing above the Lan Uchaf (the Upper Lan), you descend the steep hill leading to Ty'n-y-Gelli until you reach the bridge over the Clydach.

Stop here and look at the old house sheltering under the bridge with its feet, as it were, dangling in the river. You will see the remains of an old village which, like its former residents, has decayed. Over sixty years ago Morgan and Rachel Jones lived in this house, where they brought up a large family. They lived peacefully in this spot for the greater part of this century until, at the age of 86, death paid a visit to the quiet place and carried Morgan to rest near the wall of Gwynno's church. That was eight years ago. Two or three years later death called again and took Rachel to rest with Morgan in the lee of the church.

Eighty years on the bank and in the whispering sound of the sparkling little river Clydach with nothing but the song and roar of Nature to break the solitude! Well, were I to let my imagination run riot, I could recall a myriad of memories of interest to me but which may not capture that of the average reader! Thus I shall restrain that imagination of mine so that you can sit, rest and remain content till we take off on another journey later.

But here we are in Cwm Clydach. Turn in for a moment. An old lady lives here and it is my pleasure to introduce her to you.

'Mrs Phillips, how are you today?'

'My old legs are a bit stiff,' said she, 'come in and sit down.'

You obey and take a look at her. She has a strange appearance. Although old, she is as firm and sturdy as an old oak tree. She has a determined look with sharp, bright eyes that become rather angry when she is offended. However you sense that at heart she is good, true and honest. There is no deceit or hypocrisy here. She is so honest, truthful and loyal that she would not fear the reading of her heart by God or man. No! She is free from cant. You can trust her and, as they say in Llanwynno, 'she is as honest as an oat-grain.' Such a person is Siân Phylip, 'the deaconess', as she was called in Ystrad, for it was at Heolfach, Ystradyfodwg that she spent the greater part of her long life.

In Ystrad, almost the whole of the care of the little Methodist chapel fell on her shoulders. Yes, she was more zealous and faithful than many of the elders, both when the membership was weak and when it prospered. Her faith never failed, her patience never weakened and her generosity never ceased towards the little chapel in Heolfach. Even when they built a new chapel, she was as faithful as ever and earned the epithet, 'the deaconess'. But I can go back before that time. She was a member of the old chapel in Llanwynno when she lived at Heolfach, Ystrad. For many years she tramped over the mountain regularly twice a week for the services in Llanwynno.

The old man from Penrhys travelled with her. He was a short, strong, broad-backed man. His hair, always cut very short for some reason, was as white as snow. He was never known to part his hair but used to draw his hand over his head towards his forehead, thus serving the purpose of a brush and comb. Still, he always looked neat and well-groomed.

For many years Siân Phylip and Evan Davies journeyed together to worship the God of their fathers. Each had a horse, which was just as well because it was quite an ordeal crossing the mountains of Penrhys and Gwyngul in all weathers. Evan Davies had a big, heavy horse that was so broad and clumsy that we as children often wondered how Evan was able to ride it without splitting it in two. But Evan coped well as he sat mounted on the horse's back like a strong oak. Sometimes he put the horse in the paddock behind the chapel until the service was over. The horse was not always in the sort of religious mood that befitted the occasion. On one occasion John of the Chapel House got on his back, and so did the cat. Perhaps sensing the cat's presence, the horse became angry and made an 'unholy scene' in the chapel field. He tossed John off his back, breaking John's leg in the process and then trampled on the poor cat with the force of his hoof. But, to the astonishment of the children, the old man put no blame on the horse. 'Listen, boy,' he said to John, 'what did you do to him? You've been teasing the horse, or else he would not have behaved like this. Oh, dear, these naughty children!' Fortunately, John got better and the old man continued his religious pilgrimages for many years after.

Siân Phylip had a black mare, much smaller than Evan Davies's horse, but a very useful animal. She carried her mistress for many years through every kind of weather from Ystrad , over Penrhys and Cynllwyndy, up and down Craig Penrhewl, over Mynydd Gwyngul, all the way to Llanwynno on the religious pilgrimages Siân made. Sometimes I imagine animals to be resurrected on the Last Day, especially those like Sian Phylip's mare; besides the mare, she had a little dog who was her constant companion on these journeys. Side by side with Siân and the mare, he travelled over hill and dale, through mud and water, his zeal as strong as that of his mistress. We children always knew when the 'Fellowship Meeting' was over and that Siân and Evan were ready for the return journey, because the little dog always broke into a bark and made a great fuss.

It is easy for me to recall all these things, but difficult to think of Siân Phylip at the Resurrection without the mare and the dog, her faithful companions when she showed her godliness on her travels, allowing nothing to detract from her faithfulness. She was an example to all in the parishes of Llanwynno and Ysradyfodwg. Whoever was absent, Siân Phylip was sure to be present, listening, enjoying the Gospel and receiving the comforts that came form regular worship.

The roughness of the roads between the Rhondda and the Ffrwd never succeeded in lessening her fervour. The storms and severity of the upland weather failed to stem her faith and enthusiasm for religion. She was the old type who believed that 'he who perseveres to the end shall be saved'. She contributed much more to religion than many whose names are emblazoned in marble or on letters of brass - one whose only inspiration was Jesus Christ. She did a great deal without blowing her own trumpet and never drew attention to her good deeds. When Mynydd Gwyngul has been ground to nothing and when the saints of Llanwynno and Ystrad answer the roll-call at the end of all things, many of Siân Phylip's good deeds, of which no one but the angel kept record, will shine in the light of eternity. All the works of the saints on earth are noted by the Recorder. Then will the story of Siân Phylip's love and charity stand side by side with the love of the Saviour. 'What she could, she did.' May the last years of this old lady be peaceful on the banks of the Clydach, near the homes of Catherine William Evan, Barbara Hughes, Morgan Jones and Rachel, together with many other pilgrims from my parish and my birthplace.

CHAPTER FIFTEEN

SPIRITS OF THE PARISH

There is little talk in the parish now about anyone being troubled by spirits or seeing apparitions, or hearing the eerie screams of phantoms at night, or anyone meeting a funeral cortège at night on its way to the churchyard, as if spirits were bearing the corpse on their shoulders a few nights before the actual funeral.

These matters were talked about years ago. Many good, truthful and God-fearing men have told me of their experiences regarding such happenings in years gone by. It was common, even in my time, to hear or see a funeral passing Cwm Clydach at night, or a corpse candle coming down over the Lan road towards the church, and occasionally to hear a ghostly scream on the bridge above the house. But today nobody knows anything about these things or even thinks about them. All have vanished just like the 'Fairies' Blessing'.

Many a time I have walked from the Cwm to Ynysybwl at night, troubled and frightened, expecting at every step to see some earthly being making its appearance. Although I saw some things and heard voices which I could not account for, I have never seen anything like a spirit during my walks through the parish. Years ago it was firmly believed that Satan himself was to be seen seated on every stile on New Year's Eve. I remember closing my eyes on passing a stile on that night, in case 'the old Nick' should be there wanting a rest! I didn't want to see him and I didn't want him to see me, unless he was thereby encouraged to come down from the stile.

Edmund of the Rhiw often saw 'him' in Jasper's field in the form of a colt. However there were so many ponies grazing there that no one could ever tell whether Edmund saw a real pony or a devil in the guise of a pony. If he were in fact riding one of the animals, it would be easy to imagine that His Satanic Highness was out for an evening canter, but, if so, would it not have been more enterprising to choose a different animal from a pony in any case? Will Rhys claimed to have seen the devil more than once in the form of a big dog with flaming eyes, but Will's testimony was unreliable as he was very fond of a drop of brandy!

I once heard my grandmother telling the story of my grandfather from Blaen-nant returning from the Dduallt one night, where he had been courting one of the girls. Passing the Hen Wern (Old Swamp), Satan rushed past in the shape of a huge dog, with eyes aflame. When he reached the stile, he became enveloped in flames and burnt himself out. However, my grandfather possessed a vivid imagination, and what he saw was probably one of the dogs from the Dduallt or Mynachdy going past, its eyes shining in the dark under the shade of the trees in the Wern. When the dog jumped into the hedge, it may have made a loud howling noise which, to a strong imagination, may have sounded like a clap of thunder, causing fear and havoc in the heart of the listener.

Although it was said that the 'evil man' lurked around the Old Wern, my grandfather's evidence was shaky. But why, in the name of everything under the sun, would Satan want to go to a dark, wet, lonely corner where he couldn't frighten anybody because few people in fact ever travelled through the old Wern wood?

James of Llwynmelyn once saw the devil near Gelli Isaf, disguised as a donkey. He had such a fright that he fled for his life. However, since a donkey was seen in the field of thistles at Gelli Isaf the next morning, I don't think the evidence is strong enough to prove that Satan was so silly as to appear in the skin of an ass!

Somewhat nearer Ynysybwl than the top of Graig yr Hesg is a spot called the Devil's Chair. In shape it is something like a chair cut out of rock, quite near the main road. The explanation is simple. There are faults, according to the miners, that run through the rocks. At some time in the past, a part of the rock where several of these faults met, crumbled away, leaving a space resembling an arm-chair. Some twenty years ago I well remember some people being badly frightened after seeing a spirit seated in the chair, its bright glow lighting up the road. However I must confess that, as a mischievous imp, I had placed a candle stuck in clay on the chair that night. Thus it would hardly be fair to maintain that an apparition would be so foolish as to spend hours sitting on a hard, cold rock. Most likely it was my candle that caused all the trouble. Most of the stories of fright on account of seeing apparitions originate in this way. I must say that some of them, however, are so real that I cannot speak lightly or contemptuously of them.

Some years ago, on the Penwal and Gellilwch road, the sound of a fast-trotting horse was heard. Williams of Gelli-lwch recognised the sound afar off. It would trot past the rain-shelter of Pwllhywel towards Graigwen, late travellers often hearing the sound but seeing nothing of the horse as it passed. I have heard trustworthy men, unaffected by fear or superstition, say that they have heard this night-horse passing them many times, but despite looking everywhere for it, there was never any sign of the animal.

I offer no explanation; I simply present the facts. It must be said though that there are men living today who can confirm what I have said. No doubt the laws of nature and science can offer a solution. I am willing to concede that some men, by their very nature, have a susceptibility to an apparition or that there is an identifying between their minds and these strange events. You might say that they are nearer to bridging the gap between the material and the spirit worlds and that they see and hear signs and portents that are beyond the comprehension of every person. But any more speculation may get me into unwarranted trouble.

One of the earliest sayings I heard when young was that something lived under the Glwyd Drom (heavy gate). The old people and the children all knew of it. When we passed at night we dared not look towards the hollow bank of the Ffrwd, on the edge of which stood a thickly-branched oak-tree, covered with ivy. It is there today. We thought it looked dark and forbidding at night. If it so happened that we had to cross the fields of Mynachdy, Cae'r Banwen or Cae-Cwm-Ffrwd-bach and the Geulan after sunset, we kept our eyes averted from the dark spot under the Glwyd Drom. We believed the old saying to be true. Later I proved it was a fact. Yes, I saw the spirit that lives under the Heavy Gate. I met him face to face under the steep, hollow bank with the oak and the ivy above me. I state here openly and freely that it is quite true that 'something lived under the Glwyd Drom!'

Now I'll tell you the story. It was under the old oak with its green mantle of ivy that I began writing poetry. It served the purpose of a study. Under the sharp ridge on the bank of the Ffrwd I had a kind of wicker chair that I had made myself. At my feet lay an old hollow tree whose age no one knew. It had grown on the river bank, died, and fallen into the sandy bed of the river, which became its grave. As the 'grave' was rather shallow, a portion of the trunk remained above the water, like a reminder of past days, keeping company with the oak that still stands there waving its branches over the water and beating the drum for Rhys of the mountain. There I studied, read, prayed, preached and composed poetry in the solitude, enjoying the company of the trees and the river, the birds in the overhead branches, the fish in the water below. Meanwhile I, in my hermit's cell, believed that no one but God knew I was there. However, I found out later that my mother knew where I was and all about my secret hiding–place on the river-bank where I practised my gifts. I wrote many pieces of poetry there as a boy. I still have them and have kept them, not because of their immortal value, but for the fact that these efforts told me 'that something lived under the Glwyd Drom.'

The ridge on the bank has collapsed on to my wicker chair, but the ancient oak looks down on the place and the sad moaning of the wind through its thick branches still murmurs the words, 'something lives under the Glwyd Drom.' I heard the words many times, more than twenty years ago, coming out of the branches of the oak and the thick-leaved ivy and I decided to find out what lived there and Oh, I saw the spirit! He called me to him. He spoke to me and addressed me by name. He told me to look into his face and said that he lived there and had been there for thousands of years. 'Yes' the spirit said, 'I remember the hollow tree at your feet as a young sapling, with the thrush singing in its leaves. I saw it destroyed in a terrible storm that blew across Mynydd Gwyngul like the hurricane, Euroclydon, which wrecked St Paul's ship off the coast of Malta while on his way to Rome. I am here still - look at me. Listen to my voice, understand my speech and live to tell the story.'

His voice trailed away through the wood and its echo came again and again from the heart of the old oak. I heard it fading away in the distance, like the refrain of a hymn sung by a choir of angels. I looked up and there he stood near me between the trees, with arms outstretched. His face shone like the dawn, his eyes were beauty itself, his hair waved in the breeze over the oak-tree branches and the verdure of the fields around. The beauty of all things created was to be seen in his countenance, that of the sun, moon and shining stars, the exquisite beauty of the delicate blue sky, the glory and magnificence of the day, the grandeur and peace of the night, the glory of the heavens, the sweetness of the earth that shone in his eyes, the melodiousness and charm of all the world that were encapsulated in his voice. It was this voice at the soft stirring of the evening breeze and the slow movement of the leaves in the trees and the low murmuring of the river that said, 'I am the spirit that lives in the Glwyd Drom. You have seen me, heard me, feared me, and then admired me. You have stood face to face with the spirit that wanders through the valley of the Ffrwd, over the wild tracts of Mynydd Gwyngul, through the forests of Llanwynno, to bless its dales, to beautify the banks of the Clydach and to immortalise the hills and mountain tops of the parish in which you were born. I – I am the SPIRIT OF POETRY!!' Yes, I went home having proved that 'something lived under the Glwyd Drom.' Yet I do not know whether my mother realized at that time that I had been talking to a spirit!

CHAPTER SIXTEEN

MORE SPIRITS

The dark spirit of the Upper Lan has been silenced at last. It was often seen and heard practically every night. It would sometimes appear as a gander sitting on the field-gate or near the barn-door. People had to take turns in the house to sit up at night while others slept. Old William Morgan, the tiler, and Morgan Jones of Cwmclydach, often took turns at watching. I remember the old people saying how William Morgan used to talk about the spirit: 'Here he is again, boy; he won't lose a quarter of an hour tonight.'

Another time he would say, 'He is behind time tonight, boys; off to bed, he'll come before morning.'

They would go to bed and before long the spirit would start his revelling. He made a great noise, rolling the cheese-vats down over the steps, moving the furniture about, and generally creating a stir throughout the house. However when the occupants got up to put things back, they found everything in order as if they had not been touched. As soon as the watchers turned their backs, the whole thing started up again and the house was in uproar.

This continued at the Lan for years. Indeed I believe there are some alive now, if only a few, who remember the troublesome visitations of this spirit, and how, in the end, peace was restored.

The general impression in the parish was that there had been some injustice committed in relation to some will relating to the Lan farm. It seems that the terms of the will had not been carried out properly, conveying some property or goods to the wrong person. Hence the writer of the will had come to disturb the place. Many notable people came to the Lan to try to exorcise the spirit and bring peace there, but in spite of the efforts of priests, eminent men, workmen, and other brave and fearless men to communicate with the spirit and encourage it to talk or leave a message, it continued its evil work until life at the Lan became oppressive and intolerable.

At last the owner decided to stay a night there alone. What happened between the gentleman and the spirit was never revealed, but the trouble stopped and the spirit was seen no more. Peace was restored to the Lan. The only spirit now living there is Rhys from the mountain, who comes when the weather is angry and stormy, but no one is afraid of him. It appears that the troublesome spirit of the Lan received an assurance from the owner that the terms of the will would be carried out and that justice would be done to all the living and the departed. Like all the spirits of Llanwynno, it must have been a matter of conscience.

Years ago a spirit lived at Cefn Bychan, above the Forest Farm. Years ago tradition had it that this spirit was doing penance and had been on the bare ridge for many years waiting for some special person to come along, for at times during the night it would break out into moans in a cold, hideous and eerie voice: '*Long is the day and long is the night and long is the wait for Noah.*'

This apparition could not deliver its message nor leave the place until it had spoken to this Noah and for many generations it had been doing penance waiting for the coming of this person.

Eventually the time of waiting came to an end and for some reason or another, Noah passed by in the dead of night. Noah had to talk to the spirit, who told him his secret. The matter was settled and the spirit was set free. No doubt it was glad to see Noah but I don't think Noah was very pleased about speaking to a phantom on the top of a mountain in the middle of the night! Nevertheless the fact remains - Noah came, the spirit went, never to return to disturb anyone in the parish again.

The most rabid spirit that ever troubled the parish was the one that persecuted Dafydd Fyddar (David the Deaf) and his wife, Rachel, some sixty years ago. I don't think it was a native spirit but rather one that had followed Dafydd from over the English border. Dafydd had lived in the region of Kendle in Gloucestershire for some time, and it was there, I believe, that the spirit began bothering Dafydd, poor chap, until he was forced to confront him.

The problem was that Dafydd was hard of hearing. It was difficult for any phantom to trouble him unless he could see it. Dafydd changed his residence many times but before long the spirit caught up with him. Eventually he moved to the Lower Parish Houses and from there to Graig yr Hesg Houses, called Bwlchywig (Gap in the trees), now in ruins. He thought now that he had given the spirit the slip and was hoping for a period of peace from his persecutor, when suddenly one night the spirit appeared on the roof in the form of a young colt.

'There he is,' said Dafydd to Rachel, 'the old devil is back again; he's trotting along the roof like a young colt. I hope he falls and breaks his neck, the scoundrel.'

Dafydd and Rachel went indoors to discuss the situation and decided to ask the spirit what he wanted and why he followed innocent people about for years on end. The matter was duly resolved. They were led by the spirit all the way to a place near Kendle. Under the hearthstone in a certain house they found a box and a knife buried. Dafydd lifted the box and, at the spirit's request, threw it into the river. Thus Dafydd and Rachel were released from its scourge and peace until death claimed them. Despite this, they say that the spirit's relentless persecution left its mark on Dafydd Fyddar to his dying day.

Long ago a spirit haunted the Gelynog Wood. Many people had frightening experiences going through the Gelynog at dead of night. The huge trees, many of them great oaks, stretched their leafy branches to meet overhead, forming a dark avenue like a roof which at night made the wood pitch-dark. I know of more than one man who endured nasty frights while passing along this dark, leafy avenue. One particular man, entering the far corner of the wood from Pontypridd about midnight, received such a shock that it had serious consequences for him. The Gelynog spirit uttered such a blood-curdling shriek that the man collapsed to the ground in great distress. He got home somehow but he had to have a change of clothes. An old poet composed a few verses to commemorate the occasion, indicating that it was an owl that haunted the Gelynog. Here they are:

'The night was dark and still when this foul spirit, standing on a pine-tree's sturdy branch, suddenly uttered a fiendish yell.

The trees of Gelynog trembled and small winged insects fell helpless to the ground below where the man himself lay stunned.

The nimble squirrels fled from the trees across the fields; while the hares from every direction would flop into the ditch for a baptism.

Many rabbits in the wood were rooted to the ground, unable to run, but easy prey for Mopsy (the cat) of the Llechwen.

But how did poor Joseph feel as he passed this bold goblin? Well, not to strike an unseemly note, he got new pants from Amy!

Alas! That this religious man so weak and insensitive to the things of the spirit, should lack such faith, I'll swear on oath, as to run away from a screech-owl!'

I don't wish to suggest that all Llanwynno's spirits are like the one above, nor that everyone who saw a spirit had to change his clothes; but no doubt, if one sought the origin of some of the spirits that lived here and there, such as the ones at Jasper's Wood and the old swamp of the Dduallt, they would turn out to be owls, or the like. Perhaps these apparitions, or at least talk of them, may have been useful in keeping evil at bay and creating fear of committing misdeeds. Fear is a powerful agent, even if it has no basis. I never heard Peter Hughes of the Pandy saying that he had seen a spirit, apart from that contained in a bottle! However Peter Hughes had such strong convictions that it took something powerful to turn him from his path. He was one of the old-time giants, an example of the true stuff the parish is made of. May he be blessed with a long life. I shall say something of the Pandy, before long.

CHAPTER SEVENTEEN

SPIRITS AT THE MALTSTERS AND THE PANDY

When I write of the wandering spirits of Llanwynno, I wish to do no more than record their history. I do not attempt to explain them, nor prove the truth or falsehood of their existence. My task is simply to write down what I have heard from the lips of old inhabitants. The fact is that belief in spirits existed. They believed they wandered about in various places and haunted houses here and there, appearing at various times, and that some persons have had occasion to speak to them under special circumstances. Why did these phantoms appear then, and why are they not heard of now? It is not for me to judge. Perhaps they still appear as in olden days, but we, for some reason or another, cannot see them. Perhaps the spirits of bygone days were more superstitious. Science appears to confirm their existence, but not in the form accepted by the old people. The fact remains that our ancestors believed that wicked and troublesome spirits haunted our parish in the past.

One thing that stood out about belief in these visitations was the reality of conscience. The appearance of a spirit in whatever place was a manifestation of conscience. The spirit worried the living so that they should ponder the things of the after-life. These spirits troubled certain people or appeared in farmhouses or manor houses because of some injustice in carrying out the bequests in a will and that goods or property had been transferred to the wrong person after death. However, so many of these malpractices had occurred that it is surprising that all the spirits had not returned to haunt the people who had benefited from such unlawful actions. But I must refrain from drawing conclusions!

There was once a very wicked spirit at work in The White Horse in Pontypridd, as it used to be known, but nowadays called The Maltsters. There are many who still remember the change from The White Horse to The Maltsters. I believe it took place when Mr Eliezer Williams, the father of Captain Williams, came to live there. Long before this time, a spirit had been troubling the house and some of the residents. These visitations are still very much part of local tradition. More than one person had seen and heard him. He had a preference for the cellar. As far as I can see, the cellar is as good a home for a spirit as any room in the house, although there seems to be some mystery regarding his choice of the place. Why the cellar and not the parlour or the dining-room? This spirit was sensible enough not to go up to the attic, a place seldom visited by people, but he could have stayed in the porch or sat on one of the huge fireplaces, or taken a stroll to the bedroom or the pantry.

This one had peculiar tastes. He was a cellar spirit and his activity was limited to this place. Now there is nothing suspicious in this, since there are spirits in cellars today. It may indeed have been a wise move to choose the cellar because if courage were needed to face the spirit, there it was in the form of a tankard of beer. It would hardly be fitting to take a cup of ginger beer before talking to a spirit. Be that as it may, this spirit inhabited the cellar at The Maltsters.

Many no doubt would suggest that the spirit's choice of the cellar was just a return to old habits of the person when he was alive, but I'll make no further comment! This I will say, though. If some whom I knew in the flesh were as thirsty as in the spirit, I know of no better haven or heaven for them than to seek permission for an occasional visit to a certain cellar in Pontypridd!

This spirit had evidently obtained permission, or taken it, and was now lodged in the cellar of The White Horse. The maid there was a lively, ruddy-faced girl and one night, as usual, she went down to the cellar to fill a quart jug. Standing among the barrels, perched on top of the bracket, was the spirit. There were no signs that he had been drinking; in fact, the maid and the spirit were quite sober. She said nothing about it on this occasion, but she had occasion to go to the cellar again and there was the spirit, still on the barrel, with an evil leer on his face. He was obviously angry because she had not wished him goodnight.

At last the girl became so terrified that she would not go there alone. She and her mistress would go together, one holding the candle and keeping watch, the other with trembling hand drawing the beer. One night, after they had come out and closed the door, the maid asked the mistress if she had seen the spirit.

'No,' was the reply, 'I saw nothing.'

'Well,' answered the maid, 'he was standing by your side, gnashing his teeth in a horrible manner.'

That is how things were. For some time the maid refused to go to the cellar and the spirit would not come out. However one particular night she decided to go down, a candle in one hand and a pint mug in the other. She opened the door quietly and entered as stealthily as she could. As she was approaching the beer-barrel, the spirit blew out the candle and she screamed,

'Oh, dear, what's happening?'

'Yes,' said the spirit, 'I'm glad you asked that question and high time you did too. It is I who speak to you and I want you to come with me to Cwm Pistyll Golau below the church of Gwynno. Tomorrow night at ten we'll go together.'

So it was that the spirit met her and off they went over the River Taff, through Graig yr Hesg, towards the Glôg, over Mynachdy and the Dduallt to the dark-wooded valley of the Pistyll. There they found a pair or two of spurs, the type used in cock-fighting. This spirit had been rather a wicked old rogue at this sport. He had dressed many a cockerel and got many to fight each other, causing many deaths among them. But he had added insult to injury by hiding the spurs in a secret place near the waterfall, and this had pricked his conscience. The girl had to find them and throw them into the Taff near Pontypridd. This being accomplished, the 'old gambler' was given peace of mind. The girl, the cellar, and The Maltsters found peace. The only spirits now are those pertaining to storms and the bottles themselves, both of which still cause a lot of noise. Thus ends the story of the spirit of The Maltsters.

The spirit of the Hen Bannwr (Old Fuller of Cloth) was a wicked and vicious one. Formerly there was a fulling mill, or pandy as it was called, at Cwm Clydach, and many weavers lived there. I can remember a little settlement of several houses there, but the old pandy had gone before my time. There is a small field below Cwm Clydach called Twyn-y-Ddeintir, and on this mound the woollen cloth from the pandy was dried by the weavers. The spirit of the Old Fuller haunted this place for ages and was still there within the memory of many people today. This was not a spirit that was ever seen, only heard. He was always heard furiously fulling the cloth before a storm erupted or on the approach of any bad weather. He sat on Twyn-y-Ddeintir to work and often kept up a din throughout the night. Thus the old people knew these omens as signs of bad weather. He would sometimes come from the Twyn down to the Cwm or Tŷ-Canol or Tŷ-Draw to stamp on the earth or beat against the trees. His unearthly voices made the inhabitants came out in a sweat of fear. Many a generation went to their graves as much in dread of the Old Fuller as of death itself.

I never heard of him having done any harm to anyone, except on one occasion to Dafydd Cadwgan. The Old Fuller treated him contemptuously and maliciously at the top of Cwm Wood, jumped on his back, put his feet around his neck, bent his head down over his back, whipping poor old Dafydd all the way from the Cwm Wood to Clwyd Cae'r Defaid (the gate of the sheep field). Dafydd was a weaver and the fuller was jealous of him on that account.

The old houses of Cwm Clydach are now in ruins. The framework of Tŷ Draw is still intact, old Tŷ-Canol has gone and so has the row of weavers' houses. Following them into oblivion have gone the homes of William Ifan's wife, Catherine, and Barbara Hughes, of which nothing remains but a heap of stones. Tŷ-coch alone still stands.

The Old Fuller has finished his work and perfect silence now reigns on Twyn-y-Ddeintir, apart from the railway that has disturbed the murmur of the Clydach and the sad peacefulness of the place. The spirit of the Fuller is as dormant as Dafydd Cadwgan and Dafydd is as still as the clay soil of Gwynno's churchyard, where he and Nani continue spending their vigil in peace these many years. May theirs be the sleep of the righteous.

CHAPTER EIGHTEEN

OLD RUINS

Old houses contain a lot of interest, even if they are now but a heap of grey stones. They tell a story, for many things have happened in and around them, if only we knew. They are a kind of focal point around which have gathered memories of the old people, old customs and the old way of life, which have now gone for ever. They also take us back to early forms of civilisation and lifestyle. Somehow we feel that the old houses, the old grey walls of this and former generations are all we possess to remind us of the simple way of life lived by our forefathers.

Llanwynno is full of these ancient buildings. It would be interesting to visit every ruin, stand above it and meditate on events on times gone by. Let your imagination run free as you think of the customs, the names, and the old people that dominated them long before we were born and long before English ways had polluted the country and lowered the Welsh scene as regards house, chapel, dress and appearance! Let us take a look at some of the ruined houses of Llanwynno.

We'll start with Pontypridd. Where is Ynysgafaelon? Not a trace of it is to be seen anywhere among the newer houses there. Over there, near the house we called Superintendent Thomas's house, we can see the ruins of the old house, Ynysgafaelon, or as the old people called it, 'Y Sgyfilon.' It was once famous and much business was carried on there. Many still remember Billy the Tailor, or Billy Ysgyfelon, as he was called. He was the father of Catherine, the wife of Job Morgan. Job built Brynffynnon Inn near Llanwynno church. Catherine has been dead forty-four years and Job nearly as long. William Morgan, their son, lived to a good age and has followed his parents to the furrow of the quiet valley. Edward, the other son, has crossed the stormy seas and found a grave in a foreign land. Their sister, Mary, sleeps in American soil. All these and many more had connections with the old house, a part of whose wall is still to be seen, a monument of old Ynysgafaelon, or according to some, Ynys-y-gof-hoelion,' (= the house of a nail merchant, who was well-known in former days).

Higher up on the banks of the Taff, near the Berw (near the present Berw Road), at the foot of Graig-yr-Hesg, we see the shell of Gellidawel (the Quiet Grove), an old Welsh name, full of imagery and poetry. Yes, the Quiet Grove, sheltering under Graig-yr-Hesg. It was occupied, as I remember, by Moses Roderick and his family. Somehow it was allowed to fall into decay and every time I pass that way, I feel a longing for Gellidawel, as it was. It could still be made into a suitable family residence.

On the summit of Graig-yr-Hesg are the remains of Tŷ'r Bush (Bush House). A famous old house, it has associations with the Cefn and also with Christiana Pitts, on whose grave is the oldest inscription in Llanwynno churchyard: 'Christiana Pitts, wife of J Pitts, June 4th. 1667.' The old walls still stand on Graig-yr-Hesg and that is all we have to remind us of the life and residence of J Pitts in this part of the parish.

Saint Gwynno's church nestling in the shadow of Cefn Gwyngul
with the distant hills looking northwards towards Aberdare

The effigy of Saint Gwynno over the church porch. Only one other example exists of this saint in visual form, namely in a stained glass window at Saint Gwynno's church, Caersws, Mid Wales

The Brynnffynnon Inn (mis-spelt on the sign outside!), In
Glanffrwd's own words, 'A new hostelry was erected equal to
anything the streets of Cardiff could provide!"

Graig-yr-Hesg, a wooded rocky escarpment to the north of
Pontypridd. 'From the top of Graig-yr-Hesg you will see one of the
prettiest pictures ever seen' - Glanffrwd

Dafydd Edwards (Gilfach Glyd - Tydraw) 1801-1885

Daerwynno. Originally the only building, together with the original Brynffynnon Inn built by Job Morgan, within a mile of the church. The farmhouse now serves as an outdoor pursuit centre

The Glog. A favourite subject for Glanffrwd's descriptions. 'It's so round, isn't it? Like a marble covered with grass with sheep on its slopes'

The approach to Saint Gwynno's church
from the South East in spring time

The statue commemorating the famous athlete Guto Nyth Brân which can be seen today in Oxford Street, Mountain Ash, the venue of the Nos Galan (New Year's Eve) race held each year in honour of Guto

William Thomas (Glaffrwd) 1837-1890

The ruins of a small house are visible in the stable of Gellilwch. I don't think anyone now remembers people living in it, but I know the names of former occupants. The story is told about a godly old man who was a one-time resident. Naughty boys of the neighbourhood used to watch him at prayer and would go to the window while he was on his knees. They would then snatch his wig from his head with a yell that made the old man forget that he was praying. In this very place the horses of Gellilwch now eat and sleep, with few ever giving thought to the fact that this was once a house that contained 'an altar to the God of Jacob.'

Down in the hollow, not far from where the Cynin (or Llysnant) stream meets the Clydach, are the ruins of Llwynmelyn. This was a famous inn, a sort of half-way house between Pontypridd and Llanwynno church. Close to it was the parish road, about which I shall say something later. Many of us can remember James and Catherine with their donkey, Sharper, living in Llwynmelyn. Some may remember John, James's father, and the dog Dragon. Of John nothing seems to be known, except that he was noted for eating delicious cake. If it fell below his standard, Dragon got most of it. James, Catherine and Sharper lived happily for many years at Llwynmelyn, especially if there was a supply of good butter. James and Catherine would start eating a half a pound of butter, and working from each end and would not stop until their knives met!

Llwynmelyn was noted for its snakes. Catherine spent a lot of time in summer trying to get rid of them. They would come into the dairy, the loft, the beds, indeed everywhere in the house. I well remember seeing Catherine once taking the tongs from the fireplace, grasping a big snake with them, and throwing it out of the dairy. The reason why snakes liked Llwynmelyn was that it was warm and sheltered, the walls were thick and the roof was old and well-padded. Once they had settled there, it was very difficult to get rid of them. Today old Llwynmelyn is a heap of ruins that may well be a home for bats and snakes, causing harm to no one now.

A mile or two further up on the banks of the Clydach stood Graig-Ddu, or as it is now known, Black Rock. Examples of many places exist which have been anglicised in this way. When an inn was required to be built in some outlying part of the countryside, a sign had to be put up above the door. More often than not it was in English, since Welsh was not commonly written in those days, at least not for public signs. That, no doubt, was the origin of the name 'Black Rock.' The name has stuck ever since, though the old house has been pulled down, without a stone being left.

Going further up again on the Clydach, but not far, was the Pandy or Fulling Mill, well-known as the home of the weavers of Ynysybwl (mentioned in the last chapter).I saw in the parish registers that Peter Hughes had married Gwenllian Jenkin on December 30th. 1769. They went to the Pandy to live and it was from the Pandy that she was buried, an aged widow. Griffith Hughes married Ann Lewis on August 14th. 1806. Griffith was a son of Peter and Gwenllian and I have a clear memory of him. I believe that he was the last to live in the Pandy. Peter Hughes of Ynysybwl is his son. In respect of age he is an old man, but in energy, spirit and sprightliness he is like a boy of eighteen.

There are two or three generations of Hugheses younger than he. His memory goes back to the days when he lived in the Pandy with his grandmother, Gwenllian. It was Gwenllian who married Peter Hughes in Gwynno's church 118 years ago. Until recently the walls of the Pandy were to be seen on Clydach's banks under the great ridge that has now been cut away to make way for the railway.

Near the old ruin of the Pandy grew a beautiful laurel tree which was green all the year round, as though it were determined to keep the memory of the old house and the people. Who planted it, I wonder? I shouldn't be surprise if it was the hand of Gwenllian. But oh! it has had to give way to recent developments, for it was not there when I last passed by. No doubt it has been uprooted, thus sending one of the old landmarks to eternal oblivion.

There was another old house nearby, named, 'Y Perllanau' (The Orchards). I saw a row of new houses built on the site of the site of this house. It has a name full of poetry and beauty, suggesting thoughts of laden apple-trees on the flat land round Mr Beith's 'hotel', where the great number and the fruitfulness of the trees gave it the name, The Orchards.

Many may remember The Rhiw, or the old house that stood on the side of the road from Pontypridd to Ynysybwl, close to the new church that has recently been built. There are no traces of it now, but on the meadow where it stood, battered by the weather into a grey and neglected ruin, are long rows of houses. It was a house with a thatched roof, the thatch being so poor that you could count the stars through it. The windows had no glass, but you could often see half a dozen children's heads there, as if they were on sale, especially when strangers passed. Edmund and Mary and their many children are now all dead and the old Rhiw, like the snows of yesteryear, has become a total ruin.

Long ago a small house stood near Aberffrwd, Ynysybwl, but long before my time. Probably the present Aberffrwd house was built on the site of the original house. An old lady once lived in the little house and the story goes that she, the last of the residents, used to sit with her needles and stockings on the stone that was there for the use of horsemen at Aberffrwd. The stone, like the old lady, has now vanished.

The Creunant also has been pulled down. It was a quiet little place on the banks of the Clydach, a little way upstream from Ynysybwl. Along the river's edge was a neat little garden with a clear spring spouting from the ground at the bottom of it. It was an ideal spot for children. Peter Hughes lived here long ago; he kept the house and garden beautifully. Meudwy Glan Elai writes of him thus:

'Peter Hughes can beat all comers with potatoes from Creunant's garden; There is nobody here to compare with Peter Hughes who knows the onion's uses; for growing leeks he's unsurpassed in town and country roundabout.'

But the Creunant and its garden are with us no more. I often used to wonder how many generations the Creunant saw passing by, just as the river flowed past. Many, I have no doubt. But now its visitation has come. No one survives to hear the sweet murmur of the Clydach lapping the rear end of the house, swaying along between bush and bank. We no longer hear the voices of the wife and children as they carried milk-cans along the river-bank to the spring at the bottom of the garden. True, the old house fell, but the brook remains - the Groywnant,(clear brook), which comes down from the Dduallt through Cae Drysiog and plunges joyfully into the Clydach behind the house now fallen. What a pity these old houses are disappearing!

We come now to Ty'nycoed (House in the wood). It stood above the Llechwen on the slope of a field at the edge of the wood, within earshot of Clydach's delectable voice - a charming place in which to live. Here there was no passion or anger apart from the violence of autumn and winter storms. The steep slope of Ffynnondwym afforded some shelter and the Dduallt hill kept the winds away from the west. The surrounding trees also offered shelter while giving refuge to flocks of birds. Yes - Ty'nycoed was a delightful house in years gone by, but now it lies in ruin.

We have now reached Cwm Clydach, formerly an entire village, now a complete shell. The old houses in front of Tŷ Coch, Tŷ Draw and Tŷ Canol are all gone, and so is the old fulling-mill. Cwm Clydach was an important landmark once, far more important and populous than Ynysybwl, until the Parish Houses were built on Mynachdŷ land. The elderly people of the parish came to these houses to spend their latter days and not to the Cwm. I remember William Ifans's wife Catherine residing in one of the old houses of the Cwm. That house saw many a disturbance during her time there. Catherine was not always 'a full shilling', and when she was beset by a fit, she was more than a handful for her neighbours. She would often wander off on her own in the middle of the night with the neighbours in pursuit.

Next door to her lived Barbara Hughes, a large woman of forbidding appearance. Children were in terror of her. I wish I had taken the opportunity of taking her photograph. It's a pity somebody had not done so for future generations to catch a glimpse of how quaint such old characters looked. I would like to see a picture of Barbara in her enormous bonnet, which formed a sort of tunnel over her face. It truly must have measured a yard from back to front! Inside this tunnel one saw a big, strong nose and two piercing dark eyes flashing with wrath and anger, because William Ifans's Catherine had belittled her, or perhaps because Morgan's son, John, had rapped the door while she was drinking tea. Her unprepossessing appearance reminded one of a lugubrious, threatening cloud ready to burst and pour its contents on everyone indiscriminately. Her dark, yellow skin and her angry, harsh look with the huge bonnet overshadowing everything, gave her a weird and malevolent air, so much so that she resembled an Asian woman in a short petticoat. Being of such huge physical proportions and somewhat bent over in posture, she looked like a camel in a flannel bed-gown, while her gigantic feet rivalled oak tree trunks. I can't remember seeing feet as long, wide or thick as Barbara's. In addition, she had a beard like a man and she was no 'spring chicken' either! None of the young men of her day had plucked up enough courage to propose to Barbara, for the idea of her having to shave, the problem of her outsize shoes and perhaps her manly strength and innate sourness were enough to disarm any young man.

Time passed by and Barbara was left like a large vessel adrift on the sands, a rough-tempered old maid, ugly in appearance, an object of fear to children and a laughing-stock to the shoemakers of Ynysybwl. Nothing pleased the latter more than to stir up a quarrel between Catherine and Barbara and then watch them doing battle outside. But the old women soon saw the folly of all this and in spite of their strange looks and bad tempers, there lurked a degree of gentleness under the rough exteriors. I have fond memories of the sweet bakestone cakes they gave me as a boy. The houses in which they lived are now reduced to low walls. The spinning-wheel is silent, the sound of weaving no longer breaks on the ear and the old village is rapidly disintegrating into dust under the shelter of great apple trees that overshadow what is left of the old houses.

Close by is Tŷ-Draw, a sombre heap of debris, situated in a sheltered, tranquil spot, with a field or meadow and a neat garden.

Here lived Ifan Morgan, the grandfather of Miss Annie Williams, the famous London singer. He was a tall old man, rough in appearance, with simple habits. He was often teased by the wicked boys of the village. He believed there was no one in the country to compare with 'Siôn, the son of Morgan' in knowledge, honesty and truthfulness. He and Siôn would go for a walk along the lanes and through the fields, Siôn simply feeding the old boy with all kinds of false information. He would then go home or wherever and relate all he had been told. When he saw his listeners expressing doubt as to the truth of these things, he would say,

'It's quite true; Siôn, the son of Morgan told me and he never told a lie, to be sure.'

Siôn continued to make up lies in order to pull the old man's leg. He and his wife, Maggie, lived for years at Tŷ Draw. My grandfather had a magpie that had learned to talk and had mastered a few wicked tricks too. His name was Dick. He used to call on Ifan Morgan of Tŷ Draw, and Ifan Morgan of Tŷ Canol, early in the morning. One morning at Tŷ Draw, he snatched a lump of butter from the table and flew to the roof of the house to eat it. Ifan ran out to catch him but Dick was soon out of reach and gobbling up the butter. Ifan shouted sharply,

'Come down, Dick, you bad thief. Come down, or it will be all the worse for you.' But Siôn the son of Morgan came along and said,

'Dick will surely bring the butter back, Ifan Morgan.'

'Very good, Siôn', said the old man, as he went back into the house to tell his wife. 'Maggie, Siôn says Dick will bring the butter down. Yes, he will, because Siôn never told a lie.'

Dick came down in his own time with the butter safely stacked away in his throat! Maggie then broke his wings and he fell victim to the cat soon after! As children we used to think that this was the cat referred to in the rhyme:

'Pussy, miaow, where did you singe your fur? In Tŷ Draw cooking a nice fat cake.'

The two Middle Houses have disappeared from the face of the earth. Tŷ Coch alone remains in the Cwm - the house in which Morgan and Rachel Jones lived so happily together for more than sixty years. I fancy I can feel the kisses of the old Tŷ Draw spring touching my cheek and hear the quiet ripple of the Ffynnon y Caban (the Cabin Spring) under the lush growth of the Cwm Woods. God help me! It's all my imagination! Here am I, far from the place, on the banks of the Clwyd and Elwy rivers, far better known rivers than the Clydach, but not half as dear to me, nor even as delightful to a poet who received his first inspiration on the banks of the dear old Clydach.

The once-famous Blaen-nant-y-fedw is now a ruin, a shelter for cows and their calves. The garden, the trees, the flowers are things of the past. The home of Billy Thomas Howell and his wife, Janet, is now but *'A green floor and an unkempt garden remain with ferns upon the honoured dust.'*

The old house stood some way to the right of the road running from the Basin past Gilfachyrhydd. It was a delectable spot on the hillside overlooking the Cynon valley. The old yew tree that grew near the house is still there, looking like a grief-stricken widow, mourning for her former companions who will never return to bring cheer to the old house. Flowing past the house is Nant-y-fedw (the Birch Stream), sometimes tranquil carrying little water, at other times turbulent and agitated. From afar could be heard *'The sound of the waterfall roaring over the rock and across the pebbles.'* And on another occasion,

'Whispering a score of tuneful songs over the crystal grave.'

We must now bid farewell to these fallen houses. I have not named them all, but I turn away from these decayed walls with longing and heaviness of heart. May you, the cottages of my parish, never see destruction! Stand in the sturdiness of your old age like stalwarts of the past. May the birds nest in your ruins and the breezes of summer and winter sing among your remnants! May Nature's greenest moss thrive on your walls and may the ivy and brambles of the ages form a protective rampart around you. Stand erect in your greying years until you fall with the stately homes of the land, on the Day when all things seen will cease to be.

CHAPTER NINETEEN

OLD SAYINGS

It would be interesting to have a collection of sayings, phrases, proverbs and verses peculiar to every parish. Often you will come across sayings in one parish that are totally unintelligible to the people in an adjoining parish.

1. One such saying in Llanwynno was: *'Jarvis is most perturbed.'* This description was often used when suspicion falls on a particular person who goes to great pains to clear his name. Many years ago, but not so true today, sheep-stealing was a common occurrence on the hill farms. When a farmer once made a lot of fuss, making a great show of sympathy for his neighbours who had lost a sheep, suspicion was immediately thrown in his direction by saying, 'Jarvis is most perturbed.' This is how it originated.

A long time ago there was a farm-hand named Jarvis in Daearwynno. One day the master of the place lost a knife from his pocket on the hay-field. He knew where he had taken off his coat and thrown it down on the hay, in going to assist the labourers. He knew that only Jarvis had been near that spot. While searching for the knife, no one made more fuss about it than Jarvis. He searched diligently for it and offered excessive sympathy with his master, who was not half as concerned regarding the loss as was Jarvis. It was concluded that the fuss made by Jarvis was too insincere to be the genuine article. This is why the master quietly hinted, 'Jarvis is most perturbed.' It was later found out that Jarvis had indeed stolen the knife.

There are many colourful and striking sayings that may well have derived from this parish and others of a general nature that may be common to other parishes as well. But it was in Llanwynno that I first heard them and most often. I refer to them therefore as though they are native to the area.

2. *'Too much water on the mill'* is another of these. This phrase must have been first used long before the threshing-machine or any kind of machine was ever thought of. When someone talks too much - a common failing - and talks thoughtlessly, giving no one else a chance to get a word in edgeways (even if there was need for it), drowning everyone with the sound of his own voice, he was usually described in the jocular, yet pointed way, "There's too much water on the mill.' That is to say, 'there's too much empty talk and waste of time.' The mill-wheel turns too fast and what comes out of the mill is out of proportion to the great amount of water from the stream. The result did not bear comparison with the noise! When this saying came into play, the flour-mill, the water-wheel and the fierce running of the mountain streams were the things that accounted for most noise in the countryside. It is one of the old sayings of rural life before the railway engine began spreading smoke and spitting fire through the hills.

3. *'Only his shadow was to be seen.'* This was used to express speed. When a person is running off as fast as his legs will carry him, nothing is seen of him except his shadow. When a frightened horse rushes off into a wild gallop, he can best be described as 'Nothing was seen of him except his shadow.' When the hunter is following the hounds through banks, over hedges and across ditches, urged on by the 'Go on!' of the spectators, only his shadow is visible. There is a certain amount of exaggeration in the phrase but also a little philosophy, and I, for one, cannot condemn it. How often have we seen people or animals rush past us, leaving only a trail, and have we not been carried so very swiftly in their wake that this just confirms the truth of the old saying? Again we see only the outline of form of objects in the fields as we speed past. Many a hare has scampered across the fields of Llanwynno on a sunny day with hardly anything to be seen of it. Similarly, many a fox has crossed Darren-y-foel, past Tyle'r Fedw and the Dduallt Hill, almost out of sight, until the Llanwynno pack, close on his heels, has caused it to breathe heavily and shorten his steps. The hunt ended with a triumphant shout from the hunters. Perhaps it was so late in the day that not even the shadows of the fox or the hounds could be seen.

4. *'Dreaming of a dry summer and dying in idleness.'* This is an ancient saying that I have often heard people use. It refers to someone lazy, obstinate or stupid, or a person who has allowed time to slip by without doing what he could or should have done. Its meaning extends to include one who expects Providence to do what he should do himself. Of the origin of the phrase I know nothing, but it certainly indicates great

idleness and hopeful assistance from Providence, with little effort from the man himself.

5. *'The water under the leaves is as pure as wine from All Hallows' Day (November 2nd) to the feast of Mary (March 25th.)'* I have never heard the above rhyme outside Llanwynno. I heard it first used by Mary, the wife of Siencyn Gelliwrgan - a very wise woman. It is a perfectly true statement and it shows the old people in a poetical and scholarly light. It is a fact that the water is purer, colder and cleaner in the period from the falling of leaves to the re-birth of nature in early spring than at any other season of the year. When the earth is covered with a carpet of leaves, on top of which may fall a layer of snow, the melting snow and rain soak through the sieve of leaves till the water that flows from the springs in the woods and hillsides is in fact sweet, pure and crystal-clear.

6. *'Nine roads and a field.'* I don't know whether this phrase is used in other places, but I have heard it in the parish when the gutters have needed cleaning or when some stench needs to be got rid of. If a man, woman, or house in the district looks anything but clean, neat and tidy, instead of saying that it is an appalling state of affairs, the people say, 'it is stinking nine roads and a small field'- a somewhat descriptive utterance. In the Cynon valley there is still the common saying, 'stinking nine acres.' *[Compare the phrase still heard today 'It's stinking weather!' - author]*

7. *'A bald man never believes until he sees his horns.'* I have heard this said of a man who could never be persuaded to believe anything unless he had seen it for himself. This saying has a

tilt at the man who is inclined to stand by his own infallibility than by anyone else, and is contemptuous of anyone who maintains that his judgment and opinion can never be changed.

8. *'He is either on top of the wall or at the bottom.'* This is said of a person who cannot keep a proper balance between joy and grief. Sometimes he is radiant, living on the sunny heights of triumph, at other times he is depressed, down in the depths of sorrow and listlessness.

9. *'Wimwth-di-wamwth, a dish of pancakes.'* Only in Llanwynno have I heard this, and what a place it was for sampling pancakes and syrup! The women of long ago were noted for their skill in making pancakes. Indeed, with a good cup of tea to wash them down, pancakes and syrup were delicious. In the old farmhouses great quantities were made to satisfy the appetites of the whole family and this saying arose from this custom. Although there was little significance to the saying, it pleased someone with an urge for rhyming: *'Wimwth-di-wamwth, sypyn o gramwth.'* (*'Yum yum, a pile of pancakes'*).

10. *'Y garan gas,'* meaning 'The nasty heron' or 'The nasty person.' This phrase was often used of those with a quarrelsome disposition. When a master was reprimanding a servant, or a mother in a querulous voice was scolding the boys, or else a man inwardly called another by a contemptible name, the phrase, 'y garan gras' was used outwardly to express annoyance. After all, the heron as a bird is thin and fleshless, thus a person deserving of such contempt could be depicted as thin, depredatory and, no doubt, lazy.

11. *'A snipe at the end of his nose.'* Sometimes you will meet a man

on the road or at his work in cold weather, with teeth chattering, a pale face, his hands blue with cold and a crystal droplet (a snipe) at the end of his nose.

12. *'When you've had a good deal of beef-broth, you've had enough, but there's never enough of chicken-broth.'* This saying no doubt belongs to the farming world and was used at a time when dainty meals were rare. It was broth for breakfast, dinner and supper, made form from a huge ox, killed, salted and dried on the farm. Although it was quite tasty, one tired of it day after day throughout the year, however much one liked broth. It would have been a pleasant change to kill a chicken and put it in the pot. However there was little hope of this happening often, and when it did, the broth would be so weak that it neither satisfied hunger nor gave nourishment like beef-broth. If a situation arose, however, when a servant was obstinate or perverse and the master had to repeat the same thing over and over again, he might well say, 'When you've had a good meal of beef-broth, you've had enough, but there's never enough of chicken-broth.'

I could enlarge on this theme, as a preacher might say, but perhaps these examples are sufficient to demonstrate the amount of poetry and philosophy that lies in them.

There are also many old rhymes that form part of the oral tradition of the parish. No one knows how old they are or who composed them. They still remain as literary treasures of the years whose culture was not perhaps as wide as that of today. They were passed down from age to age in traditional manner as a common heritage of the parish, or even parishes.

Here is an old farm rhyme. I have never seen it in print and I don't know its origin, but I have heard it only in Llanwynno. It is 'the song of the cows' and was sung by a woman or girl as she was driving the cows to the yard to be milked.

> 'Away we go, away we go, home with the cows we go,
> home with the cows we go;
> There's Yellow and Ioco, Fair One and Red, Red Spots
> and Bald Spots and four like Nuns;
> The Nun and Eli and four White Ladies, Lady and
> Whitehorn, and four White-faced,
> White-face and Striped One and Tali with hood; and
> one with Freckles which must be held tight;
> Three with eyes gleaming, three very ordinary; three
> black mares, there in the gorse,
> Come altogether to the court of the king, 'On you go!
> All of you forward!
> But you, women from Tŷ-fry, never, but never, shall milk
> my cows.'

It is clear that the song ends with a challenge to the lady of Tŷ-fry (Upper House), whoever she was. The word 'nun' occurs several times in the rhyme, suggesting that the words date from medieval times, or at least when the influence of monks and nuns was still apparent. [*NB Part of the housing state called 'White Rock' located at the top of Graigwen hill is interestingly called 'Nun's Crescent' - author*]. The mention of 'hood' is associated with the hoods and cloaks worn over their heads and perhaps wrapped over their bodies. Thus a cow so coloured would be what we would describe as a 'mottled' cow.

Here is another rhyme clearly referring to an age when the daily wage or hire was less than it is today:

'Grinding, grinding, grinding hard, fourpence a day is the wage this year; If we are alive this time next year, we'll raise it to fourpence halfpenny.'

This one suggests much haste and perhaps too much toil in the smithy:

'Shoe away, shoe away, shoe away faster, I must get it done, if it costs me a pound; There's a shoe and a nail needed for the hind foot, and a shoe missing from the left front foot.'

Many years ago there lived in one of our farmhouses a woman who was always complaining that she could not eat like other people. The master and the servants would hear the same old tale every day at the dinner table: *Unable to eat, unable to drink, O! Help this poor body of mine!*

Having endured this for a long time, and seeing that she was still alive despite her inability to eat, the master decided to keep watch on her. One day, he or one of the family went to the house some time before dinner and peeped through a hole in the wall. There she was, tucking into a huge meal. The man returned to work in the fields until dinner-time, when all the workers came in. As usual, they had the same dismal moaning of the housewife during the meal: *'Unable to eat, Unable to drink, O! Help this body of mine!'*

To which the master, having seen what she had already eaten, replied: *'Two white eggs, a lump of butter, and the leg of a nice young goat.'*

So she was doing quite well for herself until she was found out! We do not know the name of the farm, and it's just as well that the lady's name is also forgotten!

Only in recent years has the word 'pudding' come into use in Llanwynno instead of the traditional Welsh word, 'poten'. Even now whenever yellow (dried) peas are boiled, the term used is 'pease poten' rather than 'pease pudding'. When the housewife makes a 'pudding', consisting of flour, milk or water, without raisins or currants, the name 'pwdingen' is given to it. Here's an old rhyme about it:

Hey, diri, diri, the 'poten' is boiling, and Jenny and Johnny are busily toiling, Searching for wood for the fire. Their mother is seasoning it with pepper and flour, she's sparing with milk but generous with water.'

One of the old rhymesters once remarked:

'The slope is very trying and I am short of breath;
Step by step I'll reach the top with my sweetheart on my arm.'

What was this rhymester's name, I wonder? I have heard the name but have now forgotten it!

Here's a verse written by Ifan Moses the elder, the father of the late Ifan Moses of Hendre Rhys. The latter died recently at the age of eighty, so this verse must have been written many years ago. I believe that the poet sent it to the first husband of the old lady, Mari of Gelliwrgan, to draw his attention to the direction of sunrise on the shortest day of the year, St Thomas's Day:

'You man from Gelliwrgan, if you're alive and well,
Go early on the shortest day to the door of the little yard.
If the sky is blue and clear and free from any cloud,
Between two sides of Gelli fields the sun will cast its shroud.'

The old man, that is, the first Ifan Moses, was the parish schoolmaster for a time and I've heard some of his former pupils say that he was in the habit of giving the children words or phrases as they left school, to be repeated the next day in English and Welsh. Here's one of them: *'Wyad a marled a neidr y dŵr'* (*'Duck and drake and water snake'*)

Farewell, you inoffensive old rhymesters; many of your names remain unknown, and the place where you now await the great trumpet-call! Some of your names were known but we cannot plant a flower on your graves since, like the grave of Moses, they are closed to view. Sleep, rest and arise with the dawn and the warmth of the Last Day!

CHAPTER TWENTY

OLD CHARACTERS

1. Jenkin Jones or Siencyn Gelliwrgan was a well-known figure in his day. He was the son of William Jones, Pentwyn Isaf, and his mother was a native of Bronwydd, beyond Ystradfellte in Breconshire. Siencyn was a big, tall, shapely man who looked like a giant. In the days of his youth few were able to compete with him in wrestling or 'fisticuffs'. He and Ifan Gelligaled once fought a tremendous contest. They were two strong, violent men and they battered each other mercilessly. Siencyn was a good farmer, thrifty, diligent and honest in all his dealings, so that he succeeded in gathering a substantial supply of this world's goods. He was fond of company and a pint of beer, for that was his usual drink, though it took a fair quantity of the brew of malt and hops to have any effect on him! He could say with the poet:

Some say I am useless and with that I agree;
Oh! That I could shed my faults and fight against the glee.'

I once remember him praying while under the influence of drink, and this is what he said: 'O Lord, forgive my sins, but there, do as you like, I've got plenty to spare with which to live as I do,' while rattling the money in his pocket. He was fond of amusing and original rhymes. During the sheep-shearing at Gelliwrgan and Nantyrysfa, he always saw that the shears kept a sharp edge. He was regarded by the whole parish as a kind neighbour, a good farmer, a true friend and an honest man. Born in 1780, he died in 1859.

2. Thomas Griffiths or Twmi Ffynnondwym, was also a well-known character and indeed typical of the people of the parish of Llanwynno. Here he was born, brought up and lived the greater part of his life. His parents were of old parish stock. His father, also called Thomas Griffiths, Nantyrysfa, died on June 10th 1810, and his mother on February 23rd 1837. The Griffiths family is highly respected in Llanwynno and Aberdare and indeed throughout the land. Who among the Methodists did not know Lewis Griffiths, one of the faithful deacons of Bethania, Aberdare, and his father, Ifan Griffiths, before him? Both are now in their graves but their memory is sweet. Everyone in the musical world knows Daniel Griffiths of Aberdare, his skills as a musical adjudicator being incomparable. The name of Griffith Griffiths of Gelliwen is well-known and well-respected among the farmers of the Vale and Uplands of Glamorgan. Their uncle, brother of their father, was Thomas Griffiths or Twmi Ffynnondwym, as he was nick-named in the Welsh fashion, typical of Llanwynno.

The family were notable chiefly for their singing. No one who ever heard Thomas Griffiths singing bass ever forgot it. He had an outstanding voice. Although his voice was powerful, it was always melodious, just like a sweet, melodious instrument. I heard him often in the old chapel at Llanwynno singing with great zest, all eyes glued to him. His voice was seemingly effortless and his manner as unconcerned as a baby. He was overcome by the 'feel' he had for the music, with no desire to draw attention to himself. His reason for singing was that his heart was on fire with the tune and the words that had taken possession of him. It was just like a musical instrument in hands that were inspired, resulting in a flood of song as natural as any blackbird in a hawthorn tree on a summer evening. He had a habit of shaking his head as he sang, more through the spiritual emotion than for the sake of keeping the tempo. In fact he was so thrilled by the tune and the meaning of the words that his head swayed like a branch lightly shaken by the playful June breezes.

Apart from hymns he also sang Welsh airs with great effect. Although I was very young, the melody of one of those songs remains in my memory. I heard him singing one night, seated in the armchair at Ffynnondwym, singing, 'Yn y gwŷdd, yn y gwŷdd' (in the woods). That was the title of the song, but I remember nothing else, except that its charm still excites me. I wish I could get a copy of this old song. I can never hope to hear it sung as it was by Thomas Griffiths.

He was also noted for his calm cool-headedness. I never saw him lose his temper nor give way to angry moods; he was always calm and dispassionate. He kept his head even when Boxer was up to his wicked tricks. Boxer was a very mischievous horse and very sensitive to being tickled. He thought that whenever anyone pointed a finger at him that he was being tickled on a delicate spot. He would rear up, toss, bite and run away with the hay-wagon if he could. I have often fallen foul of him. He and Tom, the old horse from Daearwynno, were the two worst horses in the parish for kicking and being the most unmanageable. But both are dead long ago and made their way to the place where good and bad horses go. Let us not be unkind to the dead, be they horses or not. Boxer's wickedness never caused Thomas Griffiths to lose his temper, but his favourite horse was Dragon, the old white horse, or as he called him, 'the grey horse.' I don't think the horses of today are comparable with the old type, especially Dragon; you could ride on him without any bother, he could pull a trap or wagon, or carry a load; all jobs are alike to him. In those days we do well to remember that farmers were in the business of making money and amassing wealth.

Thomas Griffiths was very taciturn by nature. He was never heard to talk to excess. He would sit in the corner quite still, without uttering a word except when necessary. In spite of that he was a good companion and a loyal friend. He was never heard to cast a slur on anyone's character and the little he said about anyone was always phrased in a favourable light. He was also a good neighbour. When the hay was safely in the ricks, he always sent his servants to help others gather in their hay. In those days it was the custom for the workers' wives to gather nuts and sell them in Aberdare or Merthyr to assist in paying the rent, etc, and Thomas Griffiths was always ready to lend them a horse for this purpose. Boxer was often a problem to the women who rode on his back behind the bags of nuts as they crossed Cefnpennar to Merthyr. Little remains of this custom nowadays. However, Thomas Griffiths was always willing to give aid in this respect. He helped many a person who was down on his luck. I hope that his sleep will be an easy one and his reward complete at the 'resurrection of the just.' He moved, towards the end of his life, to Miskin and Gelliwen, and it was there that he closed his eyes for ever.

3. One of the strangest characters in the parish was Evan Thomas of Blaenllechau. Although he died over forty years ago, stories of his sayings and his deeds still remain fresh in the memory of people in the countryside. He was a man of vivid imagination and strange moods, of a very original and independent frame of mind. He was such an unique character that it would be exceptional to come across his like anywhere. For power of expression, oaths, swear-words, extravagant and reckless ideas and also his way of exaggerating everything he said, he had no equal, even among the clan at Blaenllechau.

They say that when the hay harvesting was wet, he would talk to the barometer, which showed all the signs of fine weather, but it actually rained day after day. So, dragging the barometer outside, he would say,

'Well, come outside, you devil; so then, will you believe it now?'

Another time he and the men were working hard on the hay to bring it to shelter. The hay was dry and ready to garner. Suddenly dark clouds appeared and all the signs pointed to a thunderstorm. Soon the lightning began to flash and the thunder to roar, with the sound of raindrops being heard on the mountain slopes across the valley. Evan Thomas jumped up, grabbed an armful of hay and challenged the Almighty with these words:

'In spite of you, this will be dry, at least!' Away he went to the wooden bridge that crossed the stream between the house and the field. Unfortunately he slipped, and he and the hay fell over the bridge into the water. Thereupon he was heard shouting loudly, 'Lord, Lord, upon my soul, I see you are too strong for me.'

One can recall many things about him that, on the surface, seemed rather vulgar, but somehow, knowing him as we did, they were not so. The use of presumptuous and insolent speech cannot be justified, but somehow, one can forgive Evan Thomas and put it down to the eccentricity of his character and the wild, uncontrollable nature of his imagination. He was not an evil-minded man and was no less religious than many who used more cultured language than he. He was kind and gentle, and beneath the surface was a great store of good feeling and deep sympathy of which people knew nothing. He was one of those exceptional, imaginative and loyal Welshmen of the hills. Perhaps he was inclined to deride the arrogance of the towns, the introduction of new fashions, modern civilisation and social advancement. Nevertheless, in these matters he is more perceptive than many!

On one occasion he happened to be in a house when a child was born - a little girl. She was placed in the strong arms of Evan Thomas, he himself being the son of a widow. As he held her, he said, 'I'll wait for her to grow up and I'll marry her.' Thus it happened that the girl, Amy Thomas, became the wife of Evan of Blaenllechau. She was recently buried, ripe in years, and with her went a large part of the past, its memories and Welsh customs in this part of the parish. Evan Thomas was the owner of the land at Blaenllechau, now noted for its coal, furnaces and its dense population. Yet in his day there were just two or three houses and some sheep decking the rocky hillsides. I cannot say whether life is any better or worse in this region since the time of Evan Blaenllechau, but I think that, personally, I would be more content with the sheep and the wildness of the hills that marked his day than with the coal, the furnaces, the dust, the gloom and noise of today's scene.

4. Robert Evans of Mynachdy was a brother of Evan Thomas. One had taken his father's Christian name and the other his surname. Robert and Evan were alike in many ways, except perhaps that Robert had a little more refinement, due to his having seen more of the world and to his honoured position at Mynachdy as the chief farmer in the parish at the time. But he could be quite gruff at times and often haughty in manner. Years ago it was the custom in Ynysybwl to hold a religious meeting one night in the week. On a certain occasion a Baptist minister named Jordan had been asked to preach. Despite the meeting starting late, Jordan did not put in an appearance until near the end when Siencyn of Buarth-y-Capel was making the announcements for the week. Noticing Jordan's arrival, Siencyn suggested that he should he should speak now. At this, Robert Evans, seated at the far end of the chapel, was heard to say in a loud whisper that reached every ear, 'No, let God have the last word!'

This slip of the tongue was enough to close the meeting and allow everyone to go home early instead of being kept there far into the night!

Robert Evans was the owner of Mynachdy. He had somewhat plain features and a rural outlook on life. Like his brother, he was rather eccentric and had an independent streak about him. After his days the land passed to his eldest son, Thomas Evans, who recently sold it to the late David Williams, otherwise known as Alaw Goch.

5. Thomas Evans was a tall, stately man, of pleasing and handsome appearance. He looked so grand and imposing that he may well have descended from a line of Welsh princes. He was also a very kind man as the poor people who ran to Mynachdy with their troubles would confirm. If there was a way in which Thomas Evans could help them he would surely find it. He died some years ago and lies with his forefathers in Llanwynno churchyard.

6. Evan Williams of Aberffrwd was also famous in his day and was a very good scholar. For years he acted as one of the agents of Mr T Powell, the coal merchant. Evan Williams knew a great deal about coal and minerals and gentlemen up and down the country came to seek his advice about sinking a pit or opening a level. In fact, he was something of a surveyor. He built a house between the Clydach and the Ffrwd and in the house called Aberffrwd. He spent a good deal of time fishing and enjoying the peace of the quiet countryside until death brought the command to put away his pipe and tobacco, his rod and net and move away from Aberffrwd: *'To lie in a cold grave in the narrow bed of oblivion.'*

7. Many will remember Margaret Williams of Chapel-House, as she was often called. She was the widow of Richard Williams, and lived for many years in the manse at Llanwynno. Her husband had died of cholera many years previously. All the Methodist ministers knew her as she had been a faithful church member for more than sixty years. Possessed of great mental powers, she also had a very retentive memory. It was she who attended the Revd. D Rees of Llanfynydd when he was struck down by a fatal illness in Pontypridd. There is much I could say about her and the old chapel on the hillock of Cae'r Tŷ Cwrdd (field of the meeting place), for we, as children, always remembered her along with the school and the chapel. She would often pray in ex tempore vein under the effect of a powerful sermon. I had the honour of preaching in her funeral service on Friday, July 22nd. 1870. She was a devout old lady who took care of the house and chapel in Llanwynno when things were not too prosperous. For many years the only members were my mother, my grandmother, Margaret, George and Ann Davies and the old man, Titus Jones. The services were held in the evening.

Later a new dawn broke on the work of the Lord and at the time of Margaret's death it was shining brightly.

The old chapel where once could be heard the strains of song and praise of a past century, where Joseph Davies, Evan Davies, Benjamin Hughes, old Rhys Phylip and the old man from Daearwynno all knelt at the throne of Grace, the place where a host of souls were saved, a place consecrated by the sermons, prayers, tears and sighs of pilgrims who have now ceased climbing the rocks, has now been converted into two dwellings. Instead of sacred song and the refrains of hymns, one hears the patter of children's feet and the whistling and laughter of boys and girls who know nothing of the former sanctity and holiness of the site.

Nearby, on the side of the road, another chapel was built. George Davies lived to lay the foundation stone and there the Methodists of Llanwynno now worship the God of their fathers. In the old chapel the day school was held, Joseph Davies teaching the children there for many years. He was an old-fashioned schoolmaster, who was lame and had a disfigured hand and foot. He was generally known as Joseph, the husband of Amy, the weaver. Many a trick was played on Joseph by the mischievous boys of the area, from John the tiler up to my time. John was often playing truant. When Joseph would walk around looking for him, he would call out, 'Siôn Morgan, where are you?'

John would give answer from the pulpit, where he would be hiding, by pouring a stream of water (from the preacher's glass under the pulpit desk), on to the master's head, much to the amusement of the other scholars.

'Who did that?' Joseph would ask.

'Don't know, sir!' John would reply, sending over another stream right into the old man's face, till he was blinded with water and fury. John would be tied to the back of another boy (to guarantee stability of movement) for a whipping.

'Will you do it again?' says the indignant old man.

'Not today, sir!' says John.

'Will you do it again?' Slash, slash, slash!

'Yes, if you wish, sir,' answers John. Slash, slash again!

'Will you, will you?' At this point, John says,

'I'll tell my father, the devil I will.'

The turmoil now stopped as Joseph had begun to flag and John had begun to swear.

Poor old Joseph died in the workhouse at Merthyr Tydfil. He did a great deal of good in the parish but he left it under a cloud due to a bequest he had drawn up. He had doubtless made an error of judgement and paid for it dearly. Certainly if he were living today he would have received more respect and it is doubtful if he would have been sent to end his days in such a place as a workhouse after his long years of labour in the parish. In spite of everything, I believe that Joseph is one of heaven's princes. There was much talk of his case at the time. One commentator said bitingly of him: *'Joseph Davies, the devil's faithful servant is deep in the gutter of ill-fame'*. But another, more truthfully and fittingly, said: *'Joseph Davies, the servant of heaven, in spite of all his failings; No one's born without his faults, the best [of us] is the product of clay and soil.'*

Joseph had a dignified funeral in Pontmorlais near Merthyr, although he was one of the inmates of the workhouse. Many eminent residents of Merthyr attended the funeral. Sadly I don't think that any of his former pupils came to pay their last respects or to shed a tear over his grave. I have no doubt, however, that the angels attended with Gabriel at their head, and he, for one, feels no dishonour in hovering over old Joseph's secluded last resting-place. Let us now, after all these years, do justice to his memory. Sleep peacefully, servant of God, you were not blameless, but who, for all that, can throw a stone at you? Yes, sleep peacefully in the bosom of the angels of Pontmorlais cemetery.

'Joseph shall never walk lame again, may a blessing rest upon him.'

CHAPTER TWENTY ONE

CHARACTERS OF PONTYPRIDD

Pontypridd forms an important part of the parish of Llanwynno and it would be unfair not to say something about some of the wonderful characters of this town. I wish I had time to write chapters on them – as rhymesters, merchants, preachers, and workers of past and recent times. But I must press on and sketch an outline of one here and there, as they occur to me. As I have already mentioned the poets, I had better leave them out now. A host of names comes to my mind and the personality of many a Pontypridd person flashes before me, tempting me to give a picture of each one and spend a chapter on each picture. Here are some of them – Thomas Morris, Thomas Evans or Tom the Blacksmith, Noah Morgan of Gelliwastad, Thomas Bengarreg, Roger Jones, Bili Groefaen, Evan of the Lawn, Daniel and Evan the blacksmiths, Siôn and Thomas Llewelyn, Rosser Richard, Thomas Williams, who was Siôn Llewelyn's son-in-law – all with some outstanding peculiarity of character.

Rosser was noted for his deeply felt emotions, his fiery temper and his vigorous praying. Once he won £1 in a praying match! I think that others had arranged the contest unknowing to him until it was all over and he had been adjudged the winner. His wife, Rachel, would often burst into praying during religious meetings and was known to leap about like a young girl under the influence of the preaching of the Word. She would be so uplifted that she would sing or cry, causing the congregation to join in with her. We children would see Rosser making his customary journey from Pontypridd to Ynysybwl. He used to sit in my father's seat for half an hour before the prayer meeting. We always looked out for the black cap he used to wear. He would travel a great deal here and there to pray and towards the end of his days went often to Groeswen, where Caledfryn, the poet, would welcome him. He received little for his trouble apart from praise for his praying. He was a member of Penuel church, Pontypridd.

Another of Penuel's faithful members was Thomas Bengarreg, a rather tall old man. He was very old when I first set eyes on him. However he was full of life, as young in spirit as a youth of eighteen. I believe he was over ninety when his earthly pilgrimage came to an end. Thomas Morris was in his prime before Bengarreg, but no doubt both overlapped in time as great pillars of the church membership at Penuel. Morris was a very prudent man, a capable business man, a zealous worshipper and a deacon of Penuel. He was considered very sound in his knowledge of the Scriptures. He married the widow of Griffiths of Glyncoch, one of the most respected families in Llanwynno. Their daughter is Mrs Thomas, formerly of Lan Uchaf (Upper Lan), but now residing at the Glog and their son is Mr John Morris, formerly of Glyncoch, but now living in Cardiff.

Thomas Evans, or Tom the Blacksmith, was once a famous

character of Pontypridd. He was a preacher, a successful business man, and of sturdy, robust appearance. He travelled a great deal in Glamorgan as a preacher, but his talent was rather limited in this direction and he failed make his mark. However he possessed good judgment and much common sense. He looked at his best on horseback for when he went about on his black horse he looked like a prince. His broad, powerful shoulders and his fine, ruddy complexion made him an object of attention, especially when on his high-spirited black horse. Though he had devoted many years to preaching, the same commitment could not be said to have been made to hard study. This said, he was quite successful in business matters. His wife once said of him that she had found a way of making Thomas sleep without much trouble. 'Just put a book in his hand and he falls asleep immediately.'

In his own narrow circle of activity he was faithful. Although he was not a star of the first magnitude, within the limits of his ability we truly believe that he reflects the light of the Sun of Righteousness. If we had been forced to work at the anvil as hard as Thomas Evans, I don't suppose we should have been as physically and spiritually fit as he and his black horse! May he rest: *'Till the morning of his return to his rightful place, on the right of his Father.'*

William Morgan of Groesfaen was better known as Bili Groesfaen. He was prominent in the building trade. It was he who built the parish church at Ystrad Mynach and Penuel chapel, Pontypridd, I believe. He also built the church in the centre of the town (St Catherine's), although he did not live to complete it. This task fell to his son, William. Father and son now sleep together in the old churchyard, but their work stands as a series of memorials in the form of churches and chapels. The old man was regarded as a witty individual, his retorts being lively and penetrating. Bili was somewhat narrow in his religious outlook, especially when attending the fellowship meetings; his favourite text, which is often quoted, was: 'Do not remove the boundary set by your fathers'.

Another peculiar feature about Bili Groesfaen was that he never had any teeth, although he could chew as well as the man with the strongest teeth. His teeth had never come through the gums that cover the teeth in a man's jaws. He reared a big family, many of whom, together with their children, are highly respected in Pontypridd and the surrounding area.

Siôn and Thomas Llewelyn were brothers, both being faithful members of Penuel church. My first recollection of Thomas was seeing him hauling coal in a cart from Pwllhywel to Pontypridd. In the shafts of the cart was Fanny, a big, gaunt, thin mare that used to be ridden by Daniel Jones, of Cloth Hall, in the fox and hare hunts. Fanny's hunting days were over when Thomas Llewelyn bought her, and pulling a cart over Graigwen Hill required less speed and energy than galloping over the fields of Llanwynno, Llanfabon and Eglwysilan.

Thomas Llewelyn kept Chapel House, near Penuel, long before the present chapel was built. Nannah, his wife, was an intelligent woman, especially in her knowledge of family trees and family history of the surrounding parishes. But what amazed us as children was the great size of her nose, for nature had been very generous with this part of her anatomy. She lived many years after her husband. Siôn Llewelyn had a large family, many of whom, and their descendants, are still to be found in Pontypridd.

I suppose I should mention the name of Billy the tiler, a typical

Llanwynno man, who lived most of his life in Pontypridd. Billy was a quaint character; he spent more money on beer than many a dozen men. He would get up in the morning with the one express intention of going out to drink and come in for his meals at intervals as though he were working. He paid his bill for beer, which was not small, twice a year. Listening to Billy telling a yarn over a pint, one would think he was a foreigner, or at least speaking a foreign tongue, so strange was his speech. Almost every word he uttered was preceded by 'Said I, said he,' until a short story became a very long, complicated one, without sense or substance. I heard him tell a story of how he once slept in a strange bed in which he was greatly troubled by fleas. He took nearly half a day to relate his experiences, embellished with an occasional verse. His attempt at the verse went something like this:

'Well of all the rotten places (said I, said he) in which to sleep all alone (said I, said he, said I);
This is the worst for fleas (said I, said he); it's full of devilish thorns (Yes, said I, said he, said I).'

One unusual feature about him was his respect for the Sabbath. He never went out to have a tipple on Sunday. Instead he went earnestly and smartly dressed to public worship. I forget the two verses written as an epitaph to him by Gwilym Eilian and Brynfab, both adjudged winners in the Pontypridd Eisteddfod of 1871. I should have liked to have given an outline of some other characters that have now gone from us. Perhaps some other time!

Please do not take offence if I mention some of the successful business men of the town. There was John Griffiths of Mill Street, who began in a very small way, just like the River Severn, in a beam of light, but, like that river, his business grew until he was one of the chief tradesmen in the town, retiring long before he died, having made a large fortune. His sons are George Griffiths, owner of the Gelli pit, and William Griffiths. John was noted for his industriousness, his untiring application to his work, keenness, regular habits and care for his business. It was in that quiet diligence and unceasing toil for years in Mill Street that John made his mint, a good name, and respected position among the topmost tradesmen in Pontypridd. He was a faithful Baptist, first at Carmel chapel, then at Tabernacle. Now 'he has put this tabernacle away' and we hope that he now lives in a 'house, eternal and not made by man, in heaven.'

At the upper end of Mill Street was another tradesman, on the lines of John Griffiths and a relative too, being a zealous Baptist again - his name was Aaron Cule. He started at ground level and grew into a great oak-tree. At first his business was a small affair, his shop narrow and small, but on this foundation he built a fine, magnificent store, resembling a great London shop. Indeed this small business grew until it filled even the present wide building with stock.

The Cule family is talented and respected. Evan Cule, the father of Aaron and Moses, was a man of great gifts and much wit. Moses was given to composing verse when time permitted, but I never hear of Aaron being inclined towards a literary tongue. His Muse is business; his 'englynion' are bags of gold, and he has a store of these. He has now retired and has transferred the business to his sons. He now spends the evening of his days enjoying the fruits of his labours and contributing to the well-being of his fellow townsmen by taking a leading part in the activities of the various

Boards, as guardian and official. Like his brother-in-law, John Griffiths, he was a member of Tabernacle chapel. [*now the site of the Pontypridd Museum – author*]

Tabernacle gives shelter to many of the town's affluent people who have enjoyed the ministry of the learned Dr Roberts; others have chosen to return to Carmel, which has been re-built in a lovely spot close to Graigwen Road, between two cemeteries, where a vast number of former residents lie, amongst whom are Siencyn of Buarth-y-Capel, his wife, Catherine, and many others.

I believe that John Crockett still runs his own business in the shop near the bridge over the Rhondda River; he is a keen business man, small in stature, but shrewd and alert in his movements. He has now built a new shop and is also a coal merchant. Between all his commitments he is a very busy man. Indeed, to judge by the twinkle in his eye and his agility, he is one of those who can never be still and idle. He is completely engrossed in business, of which he is very fond. Besides, he is not troubled by the gold and silver he earns through his business affairs. He is an ardent Baptist, overflowing with belief in the baptismal creed. Crockett is as English a name as you can find, but he is a Welshman who is as zealous as he is patriotic.

Near his shop, on the bend of Mill Street, stands Griffith Evans's shop. He again has been successful in his enterprises and traces his ancestry from one of the old families of Llanwynno – a nephew of Walter Nantyrysfa. By his very appearance you can judge him to be a diligent man, fond of business, who likes a good story, is fond of wit in all its forms and as fond of money as anyone in the country, having successfully amassed a great deal! He and his son run the shop between them. It is well positioned, on the corner facing the

Rhondda and Taff rivers and the Tumble. He is a Methodist, a deacon in Penuel, and although I fear he has veered towards using the English language, he will always be, for me, a true Welshman.

Everyone in town knows the 'Silver Teapot' and its proprietor, Richard Rogers, a strongly-built man with a cheerful smile and full of zest for work. His premises are well situated near the market. Many of the women in the valley believe that there is no tea equal to that served at the Silver Teapot. Mr Rogers has been in Pontypridd for many years but he first saw the light of day in Radnorshire. His red cheeks, his broad shoulders and fine arms prove that the Radnorshire air is pure and that he has inherited a good supply of health and strength from among the hills of that mid-Wales county.

Tommy Lewis has left his boot and shoe shop in Taff Street, where he had built up a big business for many years. He also wrote many poems. Mr Lewis was an affectionate and generous disposition, but now he sleeps until *'The hand of mercy loosens the bolts of the marble door of his grave.'*

CHAPTER TWENTY TWO

PWLLHYWEL AND THE MORMON FAITH

The old house called Pwllhywel (Hywel's pond) stands near the Little Henwysg stream, some way from its bank under the lee of Blaenhenwysg Hill, surrounded by apple and plum trees. It is whitewashed, the roof being of grey Welsh stone. Facing directly south, the hill of Coedcae'r Hafod breaks the edge of the westerly winds and prevents the house from peeping over its shoulders at the Rhondda valley towards Cymmer. I remember Pwllhywel as a charming, quiet little farm alongside which the Little Henwysg flowed bearing the song of the mountains on its waves and the breezes crossing it.

Sometimes the wind would come from Coedcae'r Hafod, other times from Gellilwch, or the gap of the Cwm, or from Penycoedcae. During stormy, wintry weather it issued from the direction of 'the feet of the dead', while lower down you can be in the teeth of the south-easterly wind, bringing either balmy weather or whistling its chill, galloping angrily, or bringing a message of snow and ice on its wings, according to the season of the year.

Through it all, Pwllhywel remained sheltered, hiding among the hills to mock the gentle melody of the south wind or the irate blasts of the north wind. But industry pushed its way up along the banks of the Henwysg and its heralds dug holes in the earth to destroy the peace of these hills and dales around Pwllhywel. The result was that it acquired the worthy nickname of Cwm-sgwt (ugly valley) - a place of turmoil, coal, muck and ugliness.

A drift-mine was opened between Pwllhywel and Blaenhenwysg and a vein of coal at Darren Ddu was worked from here up towards the Carnau (Cairns). They worked and worked the place until the business had become like a horse that had broken its wind. Then they abandoned it, leaving it empty and ugly. The ghastly tip of rubbish should also have taken away instead of being left in front of Pwllhywel, a black mound like pitch as an insult to the beauty of this once peaceful valley.

Higher up, and a little to the east, is Bryngolau, the grand house of Mr W Phillips, owner of the Pwllhywel estate. He has gone to much trouble and expense to beautify the place. Today Pwllhywel is but a small house – a cottage, really, in comparison with the new magnificent residence of Bryngolau. However Bryngolau lacks the history, antiquity and memories of the older dwelling. The new house stands away from the old house with an air of superiority, like many a man with a full pocket, an empty head and no experience, looking with contempt at the village's oldest inhabitant and possessing little respect in his heart for the wide knowledge and ripe wisdom of the old man. As I looked at the two houses recently, I could almost imagine Pwllhywel whispering the old proverb, 'While youth considers, age knows', or perhaps its appearance must have suggested the sentence to me!

With regard to Pwllhywel, I could preach a sermon on

Mormonism, or the Church of Latter Day Saints. The people of Llanwynno associate Mormonism with Pwllhywel, simply because the large family who lived there joined this strange religious sect and moved to Salt Lake City. They were a robust family of able people and one would hardly expect Mormonism to capture them so suddenly and completely. However, Siôn Morgan, Edmund and Mari and her family all came under its influence. So did Siwan, their mother, who was nearly eighty years of age. Away she went to Zion, bravely hoping to meet her husband, Dafydd Pwllhywel, who had died in the year that cholera swept through Llanwynno. Forty years have gone by since their departure and many still live among the Saints in the United States. But no word has been sent to their old friends and contemporaries in Llanwynno.

It is a poor religion that makes a man forget the country and the friends of his youth. It cannot be a religion if it kills the love of your country and destroys the desire to think sometimes that 'it is good to look in the direction of home'. But never a word or a whisper has come from the boys of Pwllhywel, although they promised to write.

Obviously one can hardly expect old Siwan to write, for she by this time has passed beyond the stage of Salt Lake. She has crossed the dividing line between time and eternity, where the cries and entreaties of longing friends are not heard, nor the questions of the curious and inquisitive. But why haven't Morgan, Siôn and Edmund sent us a description of the new Jerusalem and of the rule of Brigham Young and his successor, of the home of polygamy, and of the valley of the Smiths with their dreams and visions?

I always think that a Welshman, wherever he may have settled, should say, like the old Hebrew poet-prophet who wrote of his former city, 'If I forget thee, may my right hand forget its skill.' But then, Mormonism and polygamy have taken the edge off patriotism, have killed friendship and caused the hills, the groves and the woods of his birthplace to vanish from memory like a dream that a man wants to dismiss from his mind.

Mormonism not only captured the sons of Pwllhywel, but took William Davies of Penwal; he went with the group of exiles to the new Jerusalem too. There was nothing in his nature to cause anyone to think that he would turn to Mormonism. He was slow, thoughtful, and very determined; he was what Llanwynno people call 'pentan o ddyn' (a man as sturdy as a hob). When anything went to his head, it was no easy matter to get it out again. And so this stubborn man came under the influence of Mormonism, a hot-headed believer who saw the destruction of the world near at hand, and the only place of refuge was the country of the Saints, or Elect.

He has recently died and had a grave prepared far from the land of his fathers, in the earth of his chosen country, sacred to the feet of the Red Indians. He was laid to rest with words of heresy from the elders of the Latter Day Saints.

I once remember a heated argument between Ann of Buarth-y-Capel and William Penwal at the tea table. Ann as a zealous member of the Baptists in Pontypridd believed that unless you were a member of Carmel and had been baptised by the Rev. James Richards (of respected memory), you had little hope of heaven. So, over tea in the Clotch Uchaf, an argument arose between Ann and William about the Mormons and Baptism. Although there was enough *water* in the dispute to dampen ardour, things became so heated that Ann lost her temper. William was arguing quite strongly, while Ann was gradually losing ground as well as her temper. As William went from strength to strength, Ann became more vociferous and weaker in her arguments. So, when he thought he had won and had brought Ann to silence, she suddenly raised her cup of hot tea and, instead of drinking it, flung it with all her strength at the face of the man from Penwal, bringing a halt to his argument!

I believe that the incident with Ann and William occurred just before the ladies had gathered, according to parish custom, to celebrate the safe delivery of a child. It was the practice years ago for the ladies of a neighbourhood to meet after a mother's confinement to drink a cup of tea and present gifts to the mother who had achieved such a feat as to present her husband with a son or daughter. It was ironic therefore that William Penwal received his tea, not where it should have gone, but in his face! With the sudden end to all argument, the confrontation was forgotten as the tea proceeded with praise for the baby's looks and likeness to its father. I remember that William Penwal left the Clotch that evening with a long scroll containing the names of his relatives, ready for his departure to Salt Lake City. That was the last time for me to see him, I being a young boy at the time.

The Mormons caused a great commotion in the parish during this period, chiefly because anything new always attracted attention, but also because chapel congregations saw their numbers dwindling further. For their part, the Mormons made great efforts to urge the people to flee from the 'wrath to come', exhorting passers-by on the roadside with this doom-filled message. Some of the fun-loving lads showed a desire to embrace the new religion, among them Ifan Cadwgan, a brother of Cadwgan the poet.

One day I remember running from our house to listen to Ifan Cadwgan who was preaching on Tonyrynys (the island of rough ground) in the shade of the playing-field hedge. When I got home

I received a good hiding. From then on the Saints held faint attraction for me! Ifan's 'pulpit' was a mound of earth raised from near a hedge in the field, with a companion at his side. I do not recall the exact text, but I am almost certain it came from the Book of Revelation. He spoke at length about some recent miracles and swore that he had been a witness to the miracle performed on Siwan Pwllhywel, when seven devils were cast out of her at the same time. What kind of woman Siwan was to allow seven devils to take up residence in her I cannot imagine! Obviously she and her family must have felt a huge sense of relief at their departure. Not surprisingly, Siwan thereafter was inspired to follow the Saints to their abode in Salt Lake Valley. Ifan expounded on the strange language bestowed on those who were Saints. Ifan would come out with: *'Hwffi pwffi carai mwffi, thus the Saints must reign'*

While someone else makes the claim: *'Piden hirit, Padan Aram, we, the Saints, are sons of Abram.'*

'Yes, yes,' says Ifan: *'We will go to California, for this country we must leave.'*

His companion retorts: *When comes the day of higgle-de-piggledy, in this land will be great misery.'*

The three reasons given by Cadwgan and his friend for the coming destruction of this country were: (1) The ignorance of the people; (2) The Saints had foretold it; (3) Siwan Pwllhywel had dreamt it three times. 'Therefore,' said Ifan's friend:

'Rat a tat and riti riti, hasten all to leave this country;
Rili tandem rato tinder, Wales will burn down to a cinder;
Horam poram rampidaron, flee at once to the hills of Zion.'

'Amen,' echoed Ifan Cadwgan solemnly. Upon which William

Llwynperdid went into roars of laughter, and Charles of Hendre Rhys remarked: *'All those who take burdock will be sure to be sorry.'*

At this point the meeting came to an abrupt end, amid jeers and sneers from the local lads, as they confronted the faces of Ifan and his companion which were as sober as judges. Ifan asked Tom the Blacksmith if he should baptise him in the river. 'To be honest, I'm not sure,' said Tom,' with a chuckle. After Ifan left him to think on this, Tom did not take long to make up his mind. 'Ifan, son of Cadwgan, wants to drown me in the river. No, I don't think so!' And he went off to recite the whole tale to Kitty from the Ynys. Many in Llanwynno may still remember that 'saintly meeting' in the field near the Ynys. Some time afterwards, William Rhydygwreiddyn and I went to 'play at' baptisms, resulting in the both of us falling into the river! So I had two hidings, one for getting wet and the other for running from the house to listen to the Saints in the first place!

CHAPTER
TWENTY THREE

TOMMY PENWAL

Apart from the rhymesters already mentioned in this book, the number of native poets and writers is very small. Thomas Williams, Tommy Penwal, was considered in his day to be a rather skilful poet. He is often referred to as Gwilym Llanwynno. He was a son of Evan William and grandson of Thomas William Llewelyn of Glyn Coch. His mother was Mari, the daughter of Edward Miles of Blaenhenwysg; his wife's name was Bess.

Twmi, to give him his Welsh name, lived in Graigwen for about ten years, having moved with his parents from Penrhewl Llecha (Top of the Road of Slates). Later they went to live in Penwal, and this name stuck with him for the rest of his life. His father was the owner of the Darrenddu Coal Level for years. Those who clamber over Graig yr Hesg road will know that among the trees and a little off the road near Darrenddu lies a trim little house, looking like a nest in the side of the rock with the serrated ridge behind it. This spot is sheltered from the winds by the trees and protected from the gusts of the south-westerly winds by the Lan Hill. It looks just like a thrush's nest in the bank, lonely and hermit-like in the wood below the ridge. The music of the softly-murmuring breezes provides company at night, broken only by the screech of an owl or the croak of a raven coming from the teeth of the rock itself.

Down in the valley the River Taff meanders slowly and majestically after the turmoil of the Berw cascades. The lights of Pontypridd, Trefforest and the Taff valley glow through the branches of the trees. The sounds and mumblings of the town are carried on the night breezes over the slopes of Graig yr Hesg, like the distant whisperings of spirits passing to and fro over this solitary house, tucked in to this romantic ridge on the banks of the Taff. The name of this house is significant - Bwlch-y-Defaid (Sheep's Pass). It was built by Tommy Penwal's father. It was here that the father died and from here that Twmi got married. His wife was a daughter of Mr Jacob of Llantrisant and a sister of Mrs Cook, widow of the late Dr Cook of Pontypridd. Mrs Cook is still alive and has married a second time, making her new home in distant Australia.

Tommy was a rather talented boy, playful, fond of reading and of simple stories, always ready with a witty retort, sometimes with a tendency to cast a sneer, which is a common feature and a failing among those with more than usual talent. Tommy often extracted much amusement from meeting simple folk of the country by taking advantage of their ignorance and innocence. An example of this was when he once convinced Evan Morgan that the moon had stopped moving one night as it was unable to bypass Eglwysilan mountain, or at another time that it had fallen into the Berw pool and if Evan came with him one moonlit night, he would show him the moon lying like a piece of Caerffili cheese at the bottom of the pool.' 'Dear me,' said Evan, 'I've never heard the like since I was born,' taking it all as Gospel truth!

Tommy was also rather unstable in his behaviour, his fickleness no doubt arising from his excitable nature. Sometimes he was cheerful, sometimes sad, never content to be in one place, but always nursing some trifling grievance that prompted him to move elsewhere. This uneasiness marked his stay in every place. However this did not make him bitter and sour-natured. Normally he was of a happy disposition and was considered very good company.

Tommy was a creature of such a lively imagination that the future to him was one of extended bliss, such that small birds he saw flying past were eagles with golden wings. I don't suppose he could explain, for instance, why Morgan Moses of Hendre Rhys gave this answer to his mother when he told her that he was leaving for America.

'You're running away to the White Mountain,' said Catherine.'

'No, mam,' replied Morgan, 'I'm running away from the Black Mountain!'

Tommy was quite harmless and as good a neighbour as anyone. If he had had a good education he would have made a fine poet and a more rounded person. He excelled in the clever remark and ready retort, his rejoinders resembling those of a witty Irishman. It is said that he once walked a girl home, a girl who, in his mother's opinion, did not bear a good character. For this action she gave her son a good telling-off.

'Shame on you, Tommy! Fancy going out with a girl of that sort!'

'What shame is it, mam, taking a pretty girl for a walk?' asked Twmi.

'A pretty girl, indeed,' said his mother, 'Where is her prettiness, Tommy?'

'From the sole of her foot to the crown of her head, as white as the lily, say the boys of Graigwen', replied Tommy.

'Tommy, don't send me out of my mind.'

'Well, that's what Ianto Grambo did once!' said Tommy coolly.

'What?' gasped his mother.

'Went out of his mind and came back for the same price after going out and failing to find a better place for it' said he.

'Tommy, ever since you were a little boy, you've loved teasing people!'

'Is that so, mam?' Well, I'm going out now to tease that little girl whom you and others call 'the little button'. (That was her nickname apparently).

'To tease her?' said the old lady.

'Yes, said Tommy, 'or I should not love the 'little button!''

Another time Tommy came home from Pontypridd in a happy mood. Entering the house, he said, 'Mam, Ianto Williams got drunk and slept on the top of Graigwen tonight. As I passed I could see the sow from Graigwen licking his face, while Ianto murmured, 'It's great being friendly with the girls - kiss me again, my girl.''

Tommy once grasped the arms of a leading solicitor and a well-known doctor *[in the days when doctors charged for their services! - author]*, defying them to call the police.

'Why us?' they both said.

'As you are both highwaymen,' exclaimed Tommy, 'your money or your life!'

One of Tommy's friends had just got married and asked Tommy to write a verse to suit the occasion. Soon, however, the marriage turned out to be an unhappy one and the friend returned home to his parents swearing never again to leave home as he felt he had sacrificed his own happiness through making a new home. One night Tommy stuck a piece of paper on the door with these words:

'Oh! When I think of what I are and what I used to was,
I find I've flung myself away without sufficient cos.'
He once told a debt-collector who had called at the house:
'In Llanwynno you will find three difficult things to catch;
The Hafod fox without the hounds, the mind of Twm Penwal, and
gold.'

It is said that at one time he brought a number of people to Darrenddu to see a parsnip, allegedly weighing nearly a hundredweight. In the crowd were Siôn Llwynmelyn and Rachel Rhys. When they reached the Level, they were shown a donkey-load of coal. Probably he or one of his acquaintances had a donkey with its load of coal ready for selling in Pontypridd. This was the 'parsnip'!

For a time he worked in France and letters that he wrote from there to some of his friends still exist. I include the following letter because it is so typical of Tommy's humour.

'Dear friend,

I suppose you would like to know what kind of country France is. Well, it is flowing, not with milk and honey, but with water running in the gutters which stink worse than any urinal I've ever seen. There's plenty of everything here, especially fleas! They are of enormous size. Many are killed in the hotels and their carcases thrown out, clogging up the gutters. I used to think that the Glôg hill was big enough until I saw a French flea! There's a devilish amount of gluttons here, that is, men I'm thinking of, not fleas! To eat half a ton of snails only serves to put an edge on their appetites to tackle a ton of frogs for breakfast every day! There are several Welsh boys here, including one from Cardiganshire. He is one of the most peculiar chaps I've ever met. He chews tobacco, has nightmares and is absent-minded. He lodges in the same house as me. It almost turns my stomach at bed-time to see him putting a lump of tobacco about the size of Dafydd Miles' sixpenny loaf into his mouth. He has a nightmare every night and yells out that Devil's Bridge has fallen on to his toe and 'hurt him badly.' He is so absent-minded that when he went to boil an egg the other morning, he put his watch to boil and held the egg in his hand for half an hour. On retiring to bed the other night, instead of putting his clothes on the chair, he threw them on the bed and hung on the chair himself all night. Oh! I've never seen such a soft egg of a fellow since I was weaned as a child.

I don't know when I am coming back to Wales, but I shan't stay here long; the fleas, the snails, the language and the Cardiganshire boys are almost dragging the heart out of my body. Remember me to old Graigwen and tell Dafydd Pwllhywel to teach French to Siwan if she wants exercise for her tongue.

Regards from the land of frogs,

PENWAL

PS: The boy from Cardigan has had an accident; instead of putting a ratchet under the wheel of a farm truck, he put his arm. He is now in hospital with his arm in pieces and besotted with thoughts of Devil's Bridge. I have to look after him. May God punish him for clumsiness. P.'

Lying before me now, and I believe they are in his own handwriting, are several poems which he composed on various occasions. These are their titles: 'A Song to the highway between Le Havre and Paris in France', in Welsh and English, 'A song of Praise to Daniel Lewis on opening the pit in Gelligaer district, much to the latter's advantage', 'May', 'In this world oppression will be your lot', 'The Dawn', 'Morning' (which was the winning poem at one of the Eisteddfodau in Groeswen in 1844) and 'Greeting to the Welsh Society of the Rocking Stone on my return from America.' This latter greeting refers to the Welsh Society at Pontypridd, so named because of the well-known landmark of the bardic stone circle located on a hill above the town. In this poem he expresses his love and longing of his soul for his old home, his friends, and the scenes of his youth. In spite of his fickle nature, Twmi's spirit was like the needle of a compass, always pointing in the same direction! He had a passion for his country, its language, the sound of the harp, the bards and Welsh poetry in general. This is what he says in his Greeting at the Rocking Stone:

'I departed from strangers with smiles on their faces And home I returned like the Prodigal Son

Columbia's high mountains looked noble and stately, but mountainous Wales is so dear to me.

The dear Land of my Fathers, of the spirit of song and the land of the poets, be they great or small,

So lofty in thought, so passionate their gifts; I came from afar on the wings of the wind

With thoughts of this greeting and to ask for your grace, and revive dear memories of the days that are gone.

*To see their dear country is the wish of all Welshmen, to be smiled
at by friends who would not betray:*

*The sweet-sounding strains of the harp of the hills make all who
love them as happy as saints;*

*While the joy of the Welshmen to be seen on all sides and the
beautiful songs of the bards of the South,*

*Bring cheer to the pilgrim as he returns home from travelling afar
on the wings of the wind,*

*From the lands of the west, to ask for your blessing and revive
dear memories of the days that are gone.'*

All this is delectable, tender and natural enough, as poetry goes.
No doubt the lines reflect his feelings on coming back to
Pontypridd, or on the journey from the far west. Perhaps they were
appropriate for the occasion for which they were composed, but
certainly, they do not contain the power, the fun or the freshness
that one would expect from Tommy.

The following verse, written underneath the one above, is more
reminiscent of him:

*'When I was far from home and weary of my journey,
I often wished that I could be in the parish of my birth
To enjoy a sharp, resounding kiss from a pretty, buxom miss,
And eat a chunk of the big cheese of my own native land.'*

The phrases 'resounding kiss' and 'big cheese' are part and parcel
of the Llanwynno dialect. He goes on to say:

*'There are luxuries to be had in far-off lands, and here and there, good
wine,
But there are things far better still in the place where I was born,*

I'd much prefer a draught of whey, one now and again, perhaps,
Or even a chunk of barley bread in my own native land.'

One gathers that he held Thomas Richards (better known by his bardic title 'Cydidwg') of Felin Fach (Little Mill) in great respect, because he began this greeting to him, if only consisting of the one verse:

'May your muse flow like pure, crystal waters, use your great
gifts to bring gladness to all,
And weave your sweet music into heavenly song; may the fruit of
your study excel in its glory,
Think of the strength of the hills of Llanwynno, truly poetic to sing
of your praise;
May Welshmen for ever respect your great powers, and may your
work live for ages to come.'

I could quote many more delightful verses of Tommy's work, but enough has been cited to offer the reader a glimpse of his literary skills, now silent for over thirty-five years. The last few years of his life were spent at Llantrisant. He used to travel the countryside with a bundle of 'good, black tea' on his back for sale to all and sundry. He composed a poem about the tea, which was sung and recited up and down the country many years ago, but I have failed to obtain a copy of it anywhere. Although Tommy spent his last years outside the parish, he was buried, according to his wishes, in Llanwynno. He once said that there was no place where he could rest securely as at Llanwynno, for no coal pits or railway will ever come to disturb anyone and it is not likely that any town or city will be built there for the inhabitants to trample on the graves or defile the dust of those who sleep there. As long as time exists, the hymn-tunes of the wind from Cefn Gwyngul will be heard, as though trying to lull the lost generations of the parish to a deeper sleep close to St Gwynno's church.

Well! May Tommy's sleep be easy, and, as he himself said in his poem, 'In the world you'll find oppression,' may this be your epitaph:

'In this world you'll find oppression and deep grief on every side;
Freedom from it all will come in that happy, pain-free land.
When our earthly span has ended, may God give us all the right
To live with saints in blissful peace, free from pain and tribulation.'

Nobody can end his journey through this world's wilderness with more fitting sentiments than those expressed by Tommy Penwal. Gwynno's churchyard is truly a lovely corner in which to rest eternally, where neither man nor the world's turmoil can disturb anyone. I sometimes long to rest in its shade and holy silence, when my work and my journey on earth come to an end.

CHAPTER TWENTY FOUR

THE GLÔG HUNTSMEN

The Squire of the Glôg is undoubtedly the finest huntsman in the district. He always takes the lead. Although over seventy years of age, he looks as strong and ruddy and full of life and hunting zest as ever. When listening to stories of past hunts or when following the hounds, he is young and boyish in spirit and beams with health. No doubt his life in the open air, crossing mountain and valley on foot or riding his horse over the hills and fields of the various parishes where the fox led the Glôg pack, has given him such health and strength. He has followed many a hare in its intricate manoeuvres on the fields of Llanwynno. He and his men have raised many a fox from its lair in the woods of Penparc, Tarren-y-foel and many other places. Many a fox has likewise been chased over hill and dale from morning till night, until his sonorous cry was heard as a death knell to the fox that had dared to dine on many a goose in the parish.

An exhibition of all the fox tails he had collected during his life would send huntsmen everywhere into ecstasies of delight. There was no one to rival him for his knowledge and judgment during a hunt. He had a natural instinct for tracing where the fox lay, when to cross and retrace his tracks so as to be near the dogs when the end of the fox was in sight. Whenever the horses of the other hunters were tired, his horse always appeared to be none the worse. He avoided the boggy mire and never worked his horse hard on land which would sap the energy of animals and inexperienced riders. I can remember, as a child, hearing his lusty yell, his triumphant shout, his excited shouts of encouragement that delighted the ears of men and dogs. It was generally agreed that he was a master at the art of soothing the dogs and willing the men, dogs and horses to further effort. He revelled at facing obstacles and persevering until all were rewarded by the triumphant cries of the hounds. Whatever you may say, there is something exceptional about the baying of a full pack of hounds when they know that a fox has left his lair and is resorting to the speed of his legs to put distance between him and his enemies.

To a hunter's ear there can be no harp or organ that that could fill the air with such sweet music. It is true that when the huntsman recognises the voice of every dog, he feels his heart leaping at the sound of the various notes from the musical pack, followed by the yelling of the huntsman in a fervent, hypnotic 'Amen', praising the work of the dogs, cheering the followers, giving vent to his own feelings and, at the same time, giving the 'vermin' due warning that it is not safe to eat the lambs and geese belonging to the populace.

Tarren-y-foel has echoed hundreds of times to the 'Tally-ho' of the Glôg squire; for that matter, so have all the hills and crags of Llanwynno for many years, without anyone deeming the shouts to be raucous. When his shout is silenced there will be no one to equal his capacity for awakening the echoes. My hope is that his voice will not be silent for some time yet.

I can recall many sturdy huntsmen in the Glôg. The foremost among them was Rhys Edwards, a fairly tall, thin, muscular man, who was leading huntsman for years. Rhys and the dogs knew each other and, for all I know, all the worms in the countryside knew the tread of this 'Nimrod.' He knew the ancestry of all the generations of the dogs, their names and their peculiarities. Rhys held strong opinions on almost every subject. It was a foolish man who dared to disagree with him, especially when he would spit almost a cupful of tobacco juice from his mouth and then wipe his lips with his three fingers. This was a sure sign that he had made his final statement and a hint to his opponents to be silent. As Ann, his wife, used to say, 'The three are up, it's all over.'

Who knows how much ground Rhys the huntsman had covered? How many journeys had he made up and down the parish? A map of Rhys' wanderings would befuddle the mind of any geographer. However, these long trips through all weathers, with the sound of the pack in his ears, were to Rhys but a kind of short holiday, even though they brought him the burden of rheumatism that pierced his lithe limbs and rendered him old before his time. In spite of this handicap, few people had as much fun as Rhys. Though he eventually gave up following the hounds, he continued to hunt to the end of his days. If he was in the company of a friend at the fireside, he would recount his hunting experience with great passion and enthusiasm. Even laid low in his bed with infirmity, he would love to chat about hunting until death separated him from the company of his beloved Glôg hounds and his beloved parish. He retains a part of the parish, nevertheless, as a bed, in which his sleep is not broken by the noise of the hunt, nor the tread of the huntsmen, nor the cruel roar of the mountain winds as they gallop past Gwynno's church.

Next to Rhys came William Dafydd, or as some called him, Billy Tŷ Huw, a tall, manly fellow, fond of the hunt, undoubtedly, but slow in his movements. There was not enough zest for hunting in Billy to make him a Nimrod; his emotions were too pent-up, his attitude too solemn. One would imagine he were committing a murder if he killed a fox, and transgressing the law if he hunted a hare. This was his whole disposition. He was not alert enough, nor his heart in it sufficiently. The 'quicksilver' quality was missing from Billy's make-up. Perhaps he was too tall and heavy in limb to chase a fox with success. Yet Billy was regarded as a man of his word and responsible with regard to his master's possessions. The fact is, however, he was better fitted for many other things than those that concerned the hunt. He left the hunting arena at a comparatively early age, but died before Rhys. He was a native of Tonyrefail but Providence guided him to spend part of his life among the hills of Llanwynno.

After him came Thomas Morgan – Tommy, the Glôg's manservant. Tommy was a carefree hunter with a pretty strong voice, robust to follow the hounds and zest for his work. Tommy was something of a poet and composed many an amusing rhyme on light-hearted, humorous themes dealing with life in the parish. He was a Glôg huntsman for many years and during his time I can recall some of the best hunts ever held in the parish. Some of these have become a by-word for future generations.

Tommy was notable for his enormous feet. I recall his boasting of their size. At one time news was put about that many cats and dogs in a certain part of the parish had been poisoned and it was widely suspected that the culprit was Tommy. One morning a rather valuable dog was found dead at the roadside, on which lay a thick layer of snow. Near the dog's body were traces of human footprints in the snow, the obvious conclusion being reached that these footprints were those of the perpetrator. Rumour had it that Tommy was that person. At once he went to the scene of crime to measure the footprint, and it was proved immediately that Tommy was innocent, as his foot was twice as long as the footprint in the snow. As he remarked, 'I felt thankful for my eighteen inches of foot.' Tommy's first wife was Janet, the daughter of Siôn William of Cribindŷ, his second wife being Margaret from the Graig. They lived for a time at Llysnant. Tommy now rests peacefully among the old people in Llanwynno churchyard, where many of his ancestors lie, for he and all his family were Llanwynno people.

Tommy was succeeded by John John, or Siôn Benrhiw, as the Glôg huntsman. I recall his hunting 'call to the fray' better than any of the others. On many an evening I have heard Siôn's voice being carried on the breeze as he prepared the dogs for action the following day. Sometimes his voice could be heard cutting across the early morning breezes as he called on Truly from the Mill, Tapster from the Ynys, Frolic from Mynachdy, Windsor from Nantyrysfa, Childer from Ffynnondwym, and Lovely from Buarth-y-Capel to join battle with him. His musical calls to action and the baying of the hounds were a wake-up call throughout the parish, rousing the men and maidservants and sending the children, who looked up to him as a great hero, 'cock-a-hoop'. When John Lletyturner worked in tandem with John Jones, the hunt was in full flight. The former is now dead but John John is still alive and well, caring for the sheep and observing nature in all its beauty on the lovely slopes of Cwm-ael-deg (the Vale of the Fair Brow), between Llanfabon and Eglwysilan.

John was succeeded in turn at the Glôg by Edward Nicholas,

who came to the parish from the Vale of Glamorgan at a very early age. He was a strong, active young man, on whom a day's hunting had little effect. He was so fit and so fond of his work and so engrossed in his role as a huntsman that he would not have minded following the hunt by night as well as by day. It did not matter to him whether he was on the Glôg or on Darren-y-foel with the dogs, or in the Collier's Arms with a pint, his great shouts of encouragement would surely be heard to show his enthusiasm as a worthy follower of Nimrod. I am convinced that if I were to meet Edward now and recounted with him some of the hunts we held in Llanwynno, he would have risen to his feet like a youngster, yelling his familiar hunting calls just like I had heard him so often. For warmth of nature, enthusiasm for the hunt and cheerful company and for urging on this dog and that one, he had no equal. He had spent the cream of his life with the hounds in Llanwynno and for him Paradise itself will not be complete without a pack of hounds with their melodious voices and plenty of room there in which to shout with them, till even the hearts of the rocks around are stirred into action. Edward is in his element equally with the heavy going on foot, the wild shout or the final 'kill'.

But he is huntsman no longer. Lloyd Jones now fills that role. Having been born into hunting, he is very fond of the work and has met with great success. When the time comes to write his story as the Glôg huntsman, one can say with certainty that he was not inferior to any of them in ability, loyalty and zeal.

Apart from these paid huntsmen there were others who followed the hounds just for the sheer enjoyment. One of these was William Rosser, son of old Evan Rosser, known for his praying in public. In appearance he was short and ugly; he was very fond of eating, drinking and hunting. William had never done any work for the love of it, but he would tramp the earth with the dogs and in their company he would be willing to walk the world from end to end. He was an excellent walker, and when out with the hounds he would bend his body into a stoop, squeezing himself into as small a ball as possible, so that the wind would not hinder him from going as fast as possible. Another advantage was that, being so close to the ground he could hear the sounds of the dogs even though they may be out of sight. I have even seen him lying with his ear to the ground, thus knowing the direction of the hunt, while others had no idea where the dogs were. Where William picked up all this theory about these things is unclear; perhaps nature was his teacher. He was a born hunter and although he never earned much money, he certainly had earned many a sweet night's sleep and learned of the beauty of nature and her scenery, which is more than a house full of gold to those who appreciate natural beauty.

Poor William did not live to be an old man, in spite of his life spent in the open air. Although the baying of the hounds was sweet music to his ears, he did not live to follow them long after middle age. If anything could comfort him in his troubles, it was the sound of the pack, the most musical sound he had ever heard. But Will Rosser passed away and parted company with all sounds: *'When he misses the fields and the noise of the dogs, give him a headstone with these words inscribed, 'The foe of the fox and the friend of the hound'.'*

Seldom was there a big hunt without Lodwig in attendance. He was a big, strong man, full of the spirit of the hunter. He liked gathering up all the fox-hounds of Pontypridd and bringing them to the Glôg, ready for the hunt. He was a brother of Richard Evans of Pont Rhondda, in the parish of Ystradyfodwg, but spent a great part of his life in Pontypridd. His name is included in many poems to the Hounds of Llanwynno as one of the foremost hunters of the parish.

Perhaps there was no one more fond of a day's hunting than the poet, the late Meudwy Glan Elai. He loved nature and took such delight in walking through hill and vale, enjoying the open air and the beauty of the landscape that, no doubt, the cry of the huntsman and the sound of the dogs were like peals of bells calling him out to the great temple of nature to offer sacrifices and worship in the presence of the sun, the source of light. It is said that Meudwy was once at an Eisteddfod in which the late Ioan Emlyn gave the adjudication, declaring Meudwy to be the winner of the competition. He was called to the platform to receive the ribbon and the prize. As these were being presented, the hounds were heard to pass outside in full cry, with every indication that the fox was on the run and fleeing for his life. Meudwy at once forgot the prize, grabbed his hat and went off as fast as he could in pursuit of the dogs. The hunt continued until nightfall, which was when he returned to collect his award at the Bettws Eisteddfod.

He wrote many a lively poem extolling the feats of the Llanwynno hounds, with many an emotional meeting being held at which they were read. I saw many a tear fall when he read the tender poem to the Beauty of the Lan. He wrote many a vivid poem about the accomplishments of the Llanwynno hounds under the title, 'The Orchard of Gwynno'. He was one of Nature's sons.

It is clear that all these were lovers of Nature. They were hunters, not because they were cruel, bestial, or especially wanted to kill animals, but because they were Nature lovers. No one could walk over the hills of Llanwynno and wander through its great variety of scenery without drinking deeply of the spirit of Poetry itself. Although this spirit may not reveal itself literally in prose and poetry, it can show itself in the desire to tramp across hill and dale simply to admire the beauty of the surroundings and to watch the hounds following the scent, weaving their way in search of the vermin, in accordance with the strong instinct given them by the Creator.

CHAPTER
TWENTY FIVE

ST GWYNNO'S CHURCH

Almost every chapter so far has made some reference to Gwynno's church. Any history of the parish could not be attempted without frequent mention of the old church with its large churchyard, containing its vast number of former parishioners. It is here that the inhabitants meet together at the end of their earthly journey. Here they rest peacefully undisturbed by argument, with all their differences completely wiped out. Here the relatives and the dear ones of the parish lie 'where the noise of the world is not heard'. Here the living come to look after the graves, to adorn the gravestones with fine letters and decorate the graves with flowers. Here they come on occasions to Divine Service and to wander among the graves on the dust of the generations of those deceased and meditate a little on the time which is fast approaching when they themselves will be called to their forefathers. Here they in turn will enjoy undisturbed sleep, having ceased caring for the troubles of this world and cherishing a hope of the fulfilment of the redemption of the body.

I spoke previously about Llanwynno's tavern, Brynffynnon Inn, and how it had been built by Job Morgan. Up to a short time ago this inn and Nani's cottage, (afterwards the house of Thomas Morgan) and Brynffynnon were the only buildings to be found within a mile of the church. Yes, it would be hard to find a more nostalgic and lonely spot than Llanwynno. The few residents lived among the dead. Everything spoke of death. However things livened up somewhat when John built Brynffynnon. Later on, another tavern was built, called Brynsychnant. Thus, of the three buildings around the church, two were public-houses! Often when the weather was inclement at the time of a funeral, it was a comfort to have recourse to places like Brynffynnon and Brynsychnant to go and escape the rigours of the weather outside. By today the latter has become a coffee-tavern and those who prefer tea or coffee to beer and spirits can avail themselves of this option.

Thomas Morgan's old house has now been pulled down. It has always looked rather dilapidated and has carried on its back a tremendous weight of thatch to bring warmth and shelter to its inmates. Thomas and Mari now rest in their 'eternal home' in the nearby churchyard. Mr Williams, the Glôg, decided it was high time to get rid of its heavy load of wood, clay and thatch and thus it was dismantled to make room for a neat, compact house for Thomas Morgan's son.

The original Brynffynnon exists no more and everything here now, apart from the church itself, is new. Instead of the original small building with its white walls sheltering under the ridge of the church and the sign above which was a bit too high to reach from the ground, a new hostelry was erected, equal to anything the streets of Cardiff could provide! Mr Jenkins, a worthy successor to his father, has made many renovations. It was no small venture to erect such a large building in such a spot but it has been well built. Edward, the mason, and Thomas Hughes, left us a fine memorial of themselves through their excellent craftsmanship. It is a spacious house and the rooms are well furnished. It would be an unique pleasure for the people from towns and valleys to spend a week at this fine hotel. They would enjoy the pure air of Cefn Gwyngul and delight in the lovely scenery of the uplands. Indeed I would rate it better than going even to Llanwrtyd or Llandrindod Wells!

This would be a good place to hold an Eisteddfod. I remember a grand Eisteddfod being held in the long room which was built near the old Brynffynnon inn. It was either at the end of 1868 or the beginning of 1869. The president was the late David Edwards Esq of Gilfach-glyd and the late talented Meudwy Glan Elai was the literary adjudicator. Mr Mills of Pontypridd was the music adjudicator. In this Eisteddfod Dafydd Morgannwg won the 'englyn' competition with a verse entitled 'Y Gloch' (The Bell) and I rather think I shall never forget it, since I read it at the Eisteddfod in the absence of Dafydd. This is how it read:

'An instrument musical and prompt is the bell to send its message along;
Ding, dong, come, it's time to come, and thus speaks in her own tongue.'

Dafydd Morgannwg also won for the best 'englynion' in praise of the church of Gwynno. I myself took the prize for the best treatise on 'A philosophical analysis of the different names in the parish of Llanwynno.' This was the first time for me to be awarded 'the chair'. The president announced that this was the chief prize and that the winner was to have the honour of sitting in the president's chair up to the end of the Eisteddfod. It was a splendid Eisteddfod.

Eisteddfodau had been held here long before in the time of Job Morgan. Among the poets who came here at that time was Alaw Goch. Now that such a commodious and convenient hotel has been built near the well and church of Gwynno, we should see some high-class Eisteddfodau here in the near future. I would be delighted to come and take part in them.

Now let me take the reader back many years and tell of a strange episode concerning the church, perhaps one hundred and fifty or even two hundred years ago. No one has kept a detailed record of parish events! Parish tradition has kept alive many stories that I am in the process of recording for posterity. It is to be regretted that the Vicar or some of the people had not made notes or references in some of the church records about the event that I am about to relate, as well as other incidents of note in the parish. The fact is I have never found a written trace of this episode.

Tradition has it that the church bell, the Communion plate, the linen altar cloth and the pulpit cushion were once stolen. Many of the old inhabitants testify to the theft of the church bell. One night the bell was pulled down and hidden on the mountain near the source of the Ffrwd. That spot is called Ffos y Gloch (The Ditch of the Bell) to this day. The thieves were unable to take the bell away that night , so they buried it in the peaty soil of the mountain awaiting a more convenient opportunity. After some time they returned, dug up the bell from its bed of peat, placed it on a sledge they had brought with them and started off under the cover of darkness.

As they were crossing the Clydach, at a ford close to Cwm

Clydach, the sledge was shaken off balance, the clapper of the bell emitting a loud clanging. This was the mishap that brought the thieves to justice. Early next morning the noise made by the bell at the ford was such a topic of conversation that the parish policemen set out after the robbers. Through the Cwm they sped, up to Mountain Ash, past Cefnpennar, over the Merthyr mountain to the valley of the Cannaid, where they finally overtook the thieves with the bell on the sledge. That place is still called Rhyd-y-car (the Ford of the Sledge) and the ford in the Clydach where the bell rang out in the depth of night is still called Rhyd-y-gloch (Ford of the Bell) today.

From the way in which the old inhabitants related the affair of the bell with such gusto, it is obvious that the incident has left a great impression on the people of the parish and that the tradition has been faithfully handed on to each generation. The story had not been written in any books but written on the pages of oral tradition, witnessed by the way that the names of no less than three places have lived on. There are two bells in the belfry of Llanwynno church. Whether the second one was placed there before or after this incident, I do not know. One of the bells was stolen but there is nothing known of the other bell. Tradition does not enlighten us as to whether the plate, the linen and the cushion were ever recovered. The story is indeed a strange one.

The stealing of a church bell is a novel one to my ears. In olden days the bell was regarded as being very sacred, indeed an effective instrument for keeping the Devil away and preventing him from doing evil to church members. At that time Merthyr Tydfil was rather notorious for evil-doing, as it was a town rapidly growing in wealth and population. Many there had no fear of the bell which claimed to cause even Satan to tremble. Yet even they were overcome with terror when the men of Llanwynno caught them by the scruff of their necks at Rhyd-y-car! I suppose that the isolated situation of this church of the lonely upland, away from both dwelling and pig-sty, apart from the sexton's cottage, was just the incentive that any nocturnal thief was looking for!

No doubt many graves had been opened and despoiled in past years. The custom of burying the dead in costly apparel with precious rings on their fingers proved too much of a temptation for some. For me it is the height of folly and recklessness to adorn a corpse with rings, gems and ear-rings when it is left to decay in churchyard soil. The custom has often been the cause of disturbance to the remains of the departed and that home whose peace should never be broken has been desecrated by the hands and feet of ghouls.

It seems that the farm nearest the church is very old and has a close connection with the church. Its name is Daearwynno (Gwynno's land). Why Daearwynno, I wonder? Was it here that Gwynno lived in a kind of solitude? Did he leave the place so that the poor of the parish and the church may be helped? The population of the parish must have been very scanty at the time Llanwynno and Daearwynno were erected, and for long after. Pontypridd was not yet thought of. No one had foretold the rise of Mountain Ash. Ynysfeurig or Aberdare Junction (now called Abercynon) consisted of just one or two houses. The whole Rhondda valley area as far up as Blaenllechau had but few inhabitants. Although the parish was so vast, the total population up to the end of the eighteenth century was very small indeed. I have no early map of the parish, nor any record dating from before the year 1838. The area of the parish in that year was 13,013 acres. It is interesting to note that the parish roads take up 84 acres of land

and the rivers cover 123 acres. The present population (in 1888) is 18,653, compared with 11,423 in 1878.

During my last visit to my old home I had a look at the parish register and traced the names of some of the oldest and most well-known families. Among the oldest are the Howell family. They could be traced back to the end of the 15th century. If the books had gone back further I should have been able to discover earlier references. Here are some I took from the register:

1731 Evanius filius (son) of Richard Howell, baptised

1739 Ann, daughter of Morgan Howell, baptised

1742 Evan David Howell was buried

1797 William Thomas Howell and Jennet John were married in the parish church on the 17th day of June, in the presence of Walter Herbert and Evan Howell.

The bride and groom mentioned in this last entry were my grandparents, my father's parents. After their marriage they went to live in the Cwtch (nowadays Wattstown) and there, according to the registers, many of the children were baptised. Twelve children blessed their union. The eldest son, Thomas Howell, died many years ago, the second, William Thomas, was buried a few months ago at Abercwmboi, at the age of 86. Of the twelve, three are now living – my father, John Thomas and Evan Thomas together with Jane Evans, their sister, of Melin Gaiach in the parish of Llanfabon. Although the children were born of the same father and mother, some called themselves Howell and others Thomas. Howell is really the proper name.

I have not discovered in the records the name of any poet native to the parish except writers of the 'triban' (a limerick)) referred to previously. Nevertheless some writers of the 'englyn' (a verse of four lines, each line longer than the limerick) must have lived here, because rather a high standard of 'englyn' can be seen on commemorations the walls of the church and on gravestones, some of which were composed over a hundred years ago. Here is an epitaph I found on a blue stone inside the north wall of the church:

Thomas, son of Morgan Thomas, who died 7th. of March, 1759. Aged 17.
Mary, daughter of the said Morgan Thomas, 1759, Aged 15.
'Under this stone lies lovely youth, sleeping in earth's rough bed;
Place a fearful hand upon thy breast and meditate in gentle
mood.
Here's a mirror, for every age, this fate will come to you;
Freedom from pain hereafter rests upon trust in Jesus Christ.
Life and the world is fleeting, soon to come to an ignoble end;
Now is the time to wisely choose your life in the world to come.'

Who is the poet, I wonder? Anyway they were written in the reign of George the Second and in the same year that the British Museum was opened. Seven years before, Parliament had passed the Bill changing the Julian Calendar to the Gregorian one. Eleven years before the poet wrote these verses, Great Britain had suffered from a great famine. Edward Evan, the poet of Toncoch, was then in his prime. George the Second died within a year of the writing of those verses about the children of Morgan Thomas. Queen Caroline died the same year as our own local hero, Guto Nythbrân, that is, 1737.

In those days the people of Llanwynno, like the majority of parishes, took little interest in what took place outside the parish.

Little did they know of William Pitt and his career and how afterwards he became Lord Chatham. There is no mention of any poet in Llanwynno writing a 'triban' or 'englyn' on the death of General Wolfe, who died at the Battle of Quebec in the very same year that those verses were composed on the death of the children of Morgan Thomas in 1759. Having stated that I have not come across the name of any poet native to the parish, many would agree with me, I think, that the monks were attracted to the Muse. The monks were often given to poetry; indeed, they were the great teachers of the land. They were scientists, philosophers and theologians, as well. Tudur Aled was a leading bard of his time and he was a monk. Guto'r Glyn also belonged to a monastic order and Llawdden was a Roman Catholic priest. The parishes in which monasteries or monastic cells existed were unusually advanced in general knowledge. It was thought that every parish that housed a monastery was noted for its literature, learning and superstition. The spirits and bogey men of the valleys and lonely places have been here from the time of the monks. The existence of these realities helped the monks to influence the minds of ordinary people. Fear is an effective master and, of all fears, the dread of the supernatural is most oppressive and enslaving.

However, it is still thought that poetry in Llanwynno was brought here by the monks, who supported and fostered it in every way. That is the voice of oral tradition and, generally speaking, there lies a truth behind all common tradition. There are many lines of poetry quoted on the lips of local people for which there can be no basis but that of the influence of the monks. They are too polished to be the work of the ordinary person and too local in their significance to be the fruit of the labour of any but an inhabitant of

Llanwynno. There are many triads, proverbs, verses and rhymes that owe their existence, no doubt, to the age of the monks that lived at Mynachdy. Here are a few of them:

'Fire and rain on the mound of the Glôg I send back to Fanheulog.'

This is a reference to a thunderstorm approaching the Glôg from Fanheulog and Cefn Gwyngul.

'There's the house and there's the roof and there is Will's smithy,
And there's the wheel of the Big Mill grinding corn for the parish.'
Fifteen hundred and seventy seven we first wore the mottled cowl;
The Sabbath Day is thus kept clean while people wore the woollen
caps.'

The old man who recited these lines to me was nearly ninety years old, I being just a boy at the time. The lines are interesting for two strange references, one to the law passed in the reign of Queen Elizabeth the first in 1577 compelling everyone to wear a woollen cap on Sundays and the other to the word 'cowl.' This word must have come down from the time of the monks, as this was their normal head-dress.

Why a woollen cap had to be worn on Sundays is not clear.

[Was it perhaps a symbol of making a conscious effort on the Sabbath to keep all thoughts of evil spirits at bay? – author]

CHAPTER TWENTY SIX

OLD WORKINGS

The parish has been notable for its workings from early times. The Romans had their smelting furnaces in Pontygwaith (the Bridge to the Works) in the Rhondda Fach Valley. In this degenerate age the place is known as Tylorstown. Who on earth gave it this name? I remember it as a clean, tranquil place, troubled only by the spring and winter storms. Then the Rhondda Fach River was as clear as crystal, full of healthy fish. That famous angler, Izaak Walton, fished there and had enjoyed its peaceful atmosphere, the sparkling waters and the fat trout.

The main road from Llanwynno to Ystradyfodwg crossed the river near Pontygwaith, where Pontygwaith Inn was built. Then came the railway and many fine houses and huts were erected. The peace of the valley was disturbed, so also was the water and the enjoyment of the fine trout in the limpid pools. Today the stream has lost its natural colour and is now decked in black. It has the grain of coal upon it and its fish are lost to view.

The old settlement of Pontygwaith has now become a town, a town that has adopted the name - Tylorstown. One could surely have found a Welsh name instead of this strange appellation. What yearning causes men in the heart of a Welsh landscape, in the valleys and uplands of this wholly Welsh area to christen every new place with an English name? Do they desire the changing of the names of precipices and river-banks, the woods and the fields, the crags and the streams along the wild slopes of the Rhondda? Would they compel nature to speak in a foreign language as it stretches from the source of the Rhondda to the eye of the storm over Cefn Gwyngul? Are the clear springs and rivulets of this valley to speak English and be transformed like the villages that have betrayed the name Blaenllechau for Ferndale and Pontygwaith for Tylorstown? There is no poetry in it, no charm and little sense. Yet the old name, Pontygwaith, uplifts you with its Welsh lilt and lays bare its historical and essential meaning.

It was here, then, that the Romans built their furnaces and smelted their iron. Despite the Roman presence with their Latin speech, their digging, building and smelting over a long period, the valley retained its language. The time came for the Romans to retreat to their own country; Latin became extinct; the furnaces became ruins and all was lost to society except the traces and skills of the Romans. No! The Welsh language still survived! Despite their robust language and their undoubted talents, the Romans failed to impose a new name on the place! Their memory and their iron-works are commemorated in the Welsh name of the place - Pontygwaith.

Centuries later Englishmen and Welshmen worked side by side. They made furnaces and smelted the iron, which was then carried on the backs of mules to Cardiff, Pontypool and elsewhere. All this did nothing to change the name; it remained Pontygwaith. When Izaak Walton wandered along the banks of the romantic Rhondda

River, it was still known as Pontygwaith. When the tavern was built as a half-way house between Llanwynno and Ystrad, it was natural to call it Pontygwaith Inn. When the trees of Craig Cynllwyn Dŷ, Craig Penrhewl and Llechau were felled on five successive occasions, the lumbermen all knew the place as Pontygwaith. Then along comes a stranger and in his blindness and barbarity changed the name, thus destroying at one stroke all the poetry, history and antiquity of hundreds of years.

It was not enough for him to paddle in the river and muddy its crystal waters; he must pour scorn on the language of my country by re-christening the place with a foolish name, a place consecrated by the Welsh tongue for the past thousand years. Tylorstown! Ych-a-fi! (Disgusting!) What arrogance and blasphemy! I object to this name and refuse to twist my tongue and utter such a foreign word! You poets, patriots and true Welshmen, disown the name, spit on it, but never let it fall from your lips! Why must Englishmen and weak-kneed Welshmen misname our houses and our land?

Let us retrace our steps and walk along the banks of the Rhondda Fach, not pausing until we reach Ynyshir (Long Island of Land). Ynyshir is the other side of the river in the parish of Ysradyfodwg. Although the river divides us, the English dialect assails our ears again here. In the name of goodness, what has come over the people? You would think that all was plain sailing with the name 'Ynyshir'. Yet it is the fashion now to pronounce it as Ynyshire or Ynyshigher! Did anyone hear such nonsense? It is high time that a society was formed in these areas for the preservation of Welsh place-names and to teach people to speak musically, like true Welshmen.

Nearby is a famous landmark, formerly called by the Welsh name Maendy (Stone House). However the tongues of this generation seem to have grown smaller and they can manage only Maindy! Open your mouths! Twist your tongues! Take a little Welsh pride and say clearly with wide–open mouths - MAENDY.

Come with me now to Porth; no, not Porth, says the mercenary tongue of this modern age, but Porthe (to rhyme with the English word 'forth'). To pronounce it thus, in the long English fashion, is, to put it bluntly, quite misguided. What perversion of the language and land of our ancestors, while turning one's back on the words of the prophet-bard from the hills: *'A grand language, and one to take to heaven.'*

We stand for a moment near the residence of that famous doctor, Henry Naunton Davies Esq, a fine Welshman, fond of the language and literature, and the most experienced doctor in the country. His fame was widespread. If any relative of mine required a consultation on account of illness and I had permission to give my opinion, I would whisper the name of Dr Davies of Cymmer before any other doctor in the land. His house was near Pont-y-Cymmer, not far from the home of the late talented bard, Meudwy Glan Elai. Indeed Dr Davies was very fond of the poet's company. He has often taken a delight in an 'englyn' or a clever story, composed by Meudwy, and no one is more keen than he to see the poet's works published.

We leave Porth and pass Llwyncelyn pit, over the Nyth-Brân meadow to the Hafod pit, near Tarren y Pistyll. Little do the peaceful inhabitants of Cwm George, the Hafod and Tarren y Pistyll know that in this spot were made the sharp pikes used by the Chartists when they revolted at Newport in 1836. There was a coal level somewhere under the Darren and in the smithy belonging to this level were forged many of the weapons of war with which the Chartists intended terrifying and destroying their enemies. The weapon made at the Hafod pit was a kind of three-pronged fork. These forks seemed to me most unsuitable for the purpose intended.

Ynys-yr-hafod has retained its Welsh quality. You men of the Hafod (Trehafod, nowadays) deserve praise for avoiding the use of English in your district. But remember that the pulpit of Twm Ifan Prys is not far. Look in the direction of the summit of Werfa Ddu, towards Gelliwion Mountain in Coedcae Wood. It is there that you will see the pulpit from which Twm uttered some of his strange prophecies. Having passed Gyfeillion, we pause to look at the Rhondda whirlpool, which was once a famous landmark. The water fell into it rock by rock and in its depths the waves fought in their haste to escape from their narrow prison. Restrained in their mad progress, they swirled to and fro, embittered and wild, till the foam was churned as white as milk.

In days gone by there was something poetic about this Rhondda waterfall. At that time, the salmon would come up the Rhondda River and I have indeed heard that the owners of the land, the Morgan family of the Hafod, used to place baskets in the pool to catch the salmon. It was not an easy task for a salmon to pass through the pool, facing, as it did, the wrath of the waterfall to leap up over the rocks, but it was, more often than not, successfully accomplished. The baskets were arranged in such a way that, as they slipped back from the lip of the rock, the fish were trapped and remained until they were collected. Rumour has it that many a man, passing the place early in the morning before the basket-owners had turned in their beds, took pity on the salmon and carried them home – for the pot! The motive was they might as well boil on the fire as linger in a basket in the pool. Today no salmon is to be seen. Not one has been sighted for years; neither is it likely until the coal-pits have been swept away, together with all the mills between the Rhondda and the sea.

[The salmon have returned to the area now of course - author]

The whirlpool was once bigger than it is now. Coal now forms the previous bed occupied by the salmon and smothers the noise of the waves at the bottom. Commerce has planted its hoof on the romantic story of the Pool. Its song is silenced, a song brought into being when the doors of the Rhondda were opened and the hidden waters of the hillsides rushed towards Cardiff. The goddess of coal sat upon the banks of the whirlpool, polluting it to blackness. Even to this day the pool has never regained its former crystal clearness.

The Great Western Colliery now occupies this site. It was formerly known as Calvert's Pit but passed from his hands to the Great Western Company. Steam coal is produced. It is heartening to hear that this pit may become one of the finest in the country. *[It is now the site of the acclaimed Rhondda Heritage Centre – author]* If this turns out to be so, the owners will be well rewarded for their labours and the expense incurred. They say that the shares are rising rapidly. This pit is supervised by a man who has worked his way from a workman to the top of the ladder. Nothing gives me greater pleasure than to see someone getting on as a result of his own efforts and sterling work. You can be sure that when a man has left behind the mandrel and become an important official, filling the post to the satisfaction of the employers, to the benefit of the workmen and with credit to himself, then there is something more than name, appearance, talk, boast and selfishness behind his promotion.

Mr Thomas Williams, manager of the Great Western Pit, is a very able man who has gradually climbed up the rungs of the ladder of experience, finally reaching a high and worthy position. A man of this type adds dignity to the workers, is a treasure to the master, brings honour to the neighbourhood and is a crown of joy to his friends and family. Mr Williams is known for his depth of thought, shrewdness, wisdom and thoroughly sound common sense. Added to these qualities one finds wide knowledge and experience; it is no wonder he has excelled as a manager at the Great Western.

We now turn upwards and pass Troedrhiwtrwyn to the valley of Pwll Hywel, or to use its former name, Cwm Sgwt. The pit was opened by the able Eos Rhondda. All the coal seems to have been worked out now; the drift is idle and the level empty. Near this pit in olden days was an old house called Ty'n-y-Graig. Morgan of Blaenhenwysg and his family lived here. To be precise, here lived Aunt Bess of Blaenhenwysg, her husband, Edward, and their children, Morgan Miles of Gellifynaches (Nun's Grove), Dafydd and Edward Miles, one of Pontypridd's earliest school masters, Catherine, first wife of Siôn Llewelyn, together with Mari and Sioned, their sisters. They have all been dead these many years.

Sadly the mighty spring of Ty'n-y-Graig has been buried under an enormous rubbish tip from Pwll Hywel pit. Although buried, it has not been destroyed. In spite of the mountain of waste material, it gushes out somewhere, sweetly giving vent to its resurrection as it joins the Henwysg stream. Just like this spring, Aunt Bess and her family will come forth unblemished and enduring with all the Blessed at the Resurrection.

Here is Blaenhenwysg, the old home of Siôn William and Nanna, his wife. I remember being taken hand in hand by Dafydd, their son, all the way from Fanheulog chapel on Sunday to have lunch with them. I was very young at that time and had never been out of sight of the chimney smoke of my home. That was my first visit to Blaenhenwysg. Dafydd emigrated to Australia and there found a grave among strangers many years ago. But the family of Siôn and Nanna is still represented by Edward Williams and his large, respected family, now at Cribyn-dŷ.

I know of no better example of a patriotic Welshman than Edward. Always brimming over with fun and good humour, some of his yarns may be rather crude and forthright, but they were never without meaning or a pointed application. Never does he use noble language to tell his story, but he uses gentle, refined words. This style only draws out his nature and Welsh rural upbringing more clearly and marks him as a personality. A parish teeming with people like Edward Williams would be boring, but to see and hear an individual of his type is a delight and an enjoyment. I remember Benjamin Hughes once making a comment about old Hywel from the Bwllfa, that he was sure that the Creator would never dream of making more than one of his type. Having seen his untidy hair, his slovenly appearance, one eye with a pronounced squint and dressed in a kind of white smock, accompanied by a long-haired sheepdog at his heels, I was bound to agree that one Hywel from the Bwllfa was enough! I don't say that one Edward of Cribyn-dŷ is enough, but a crowd of his kind would change an exceptional character into a common one.

Benjamin Hughes lies with his fathers in Llanwynno. The Hughes family came to the parish from Ireland some centuries ago. They are still among us, much respected and prosperous. Originally they were turners, their first home being still called Lletty Turner. They have been carpenters now for many years, one generation after the other. Gruffudd Hughes has carried out a lot of work up and down the parish, as has his son, Benny, after him. Benny was one of the children of the religious revival that took place about thirty years ago in South Wales. When the revival reached Llanwynno, the members of Bethel Chapel (Fanheulog) were very few and almost too weak a congregation to keep the church alive. Benny Hughes was the first to be accepted as a new member at the outset of the Revival. What a productive sheaf of the first crop he turned out to be. He was foremost in commitment, to be followed by a large number of converts, remaining a faithful member of Bethel up to his death a few years ago. He was gifted in offering prayer in public. Indeed, had he received early training, he would have made a huge contribution to the Christian community. As it was, he showed great power and originality in public worship. As the parish carpenter, this mantle fell to his son, Thomas, who inherited his father's manual talents in great measure. But the mantle of Methodism went elsewhere, for Thomas returned to the parish church, the blessed place of his ancestors.

CHAPTER
TWENTY SEVEN

SPRINGS AND WELLS

Often I have heard the people of yesteryear boast that Llanwynno has been more abundantly blessed with springs than almost any parish in Glamorgan and that the pure, health-giving waters are free for both humans and animals to enjoy. *'This fine sweet splendid element, costing nothing, free to all.'*

Indeed the springs and wells were so strong, so clean, so abundant, that it was no wonder that the old inhabitants thought so highly of them! Sadly, today things are so different. Many of these crystal springs that bubbled out from hillsides or from the temples of stone, or else from the pure forests for which the parish was famous, have now vanished and are as dried up as the biblical River Kedron in mid-summer. The springs of Llanwynno drying up, you say? Yes, very rapidly so in every corner of the parish. I walked in the spirit one evening through the parish, from place to place, from mound to mound, from hollow to hollow, all alone. The sun had bestowed its parting kiss upon the Glôg, the Dduallt Hill, and Disgwylfa, and had now sunk below the horizon.

CHAPTER TWENTY SEVEN

'Twilight casts its slanting shadows o'er the sun's bright face,
While gentle breeze and crystal grass repair to bed below.
The shimmering heat of day has brought enchanting sleep;
And down he sinks into the night, benumbed, to dreamy slumber.'

The evening breeze lightly shook the twigs of the yew tree near the church and the Clydach sang its delightful night-time music in the hollow. The air was typically Welsh, so tender yet so mighty, even heavenly, down there in the dark valley, below the tranquil refuge of the dead. Yes, may the Pistyll (Waterfall) always ring out its old Welsh tunes in the deep dell. I wonder if it will be stilled when the water is dried up in the heat of the Last Day. I was enjoying the peace of this particular evening, while night rapidly drew the curtains on me and this corner of the earth, when I suddenly thought I heard the sound of voices not far away. Who could possibly be there? The voices seemed familiar. Yet, if truth be told, they belonged to men and women who had died many years ago!

What I heard that night on my journey in the spirit was a conversation between the spirits of those long ago characters. I could hear Guto Nythbrân saying, 'When I pursued the sheep along the slopes from Mynydd Gwyngul down to the Hafod and Graigwen, the springs and wells were as numerous as the stars and so sparkling a sight. There was no shortage of water in both summer and winter. Water will run from the Hafod hillside as long as dew and rain continue to fall.'

'Oh,' said Evan Blaenllechau, 'short of water, while we live among springs and rushes, the idea is preposterous! Why do you think that Blaenllechau, Daearwynno and other farms have to feed the cattle with chaff in winter? The fact is there's too much water everywhere - peat-land clogged with water, field after field with water up to the ankles. Let's be honest, there's no such thing as a shortage of water in a place where farm-servants' feet have waded through the stuff in the countryside for so long.'

'Never!' said Williams the Glôg, 'not while the spring runs under the house! It guarantees enough water for the whole country and, what's more, it's the coldest and purest water in the world!'

'Good heavens,' said Walter Nantyrysfa, 'There's enough water lying in the ditches of the Great Meadow to drown all the sheep of Daearwynno, and some of the wells of Mynydd Bach have never ceased to flow. If only you could dam all the water around Nantyrysfa, you could sail a ship on it - Enough water, indeed! If everything else were as plentiful, some of us would be in clover.'

'But,' replied Morgan Tydraw, 'that's just what they are complaining about. For myself, I can hardly imagine the wells and springs drying up. I have seen the Lan spring flowing as wide as a man's girth and the one at the Hafod has enough force in it to turn a mill-wheel.' 'Quite right, 'declared Ifan Moses, 'and what about the well at Hendre Rhys? That's been running since the days of Adam and it has quenched the thirst of all the Hafod animals for ages without slowing up, and anyone who doubts this is making a huge mistake. What do you say, Rhys and Als?'

'I can tell you, I saw enough water,' replied Rhys, 'too much, I reckon, when the Ffrwd broke its banks carrying all in its wake through my shop.'

'Yes,' said Als, and what about the way it took one of the Ynys pigs during a flood and two of my ducks down as far as the horse-pool, and me finding them floating in it, as dead as dodos. It was the force of water that got the better of them. You can't tell me there's not enough water in the Ffrwd after rain.'

'I find there's water, water, everywhere,' joined in Lewis the Forest. 'If the same share of milk, cream and beer had come my way in Llanwynno, I would have been jumping for joy, I can tell you; those who dare to say that Llanwynno has a water problem have water on the brain! Yes, water up to the neck! - Good Lord, deliver us!'

'You gullible creature!' cried Billy Rhydygwreiddyn, 'don't you know that there's a change afoot in the parish?' Don't you know that such a thing as coal is being worked, and that the springs are being sucked down to the empty spaces in the ground?'

'Oh, I've known that for a long time,' said Jackie Gellilwch. 'Take Darrenddu Level, for instance; it has nearly dried up the land at Gellilwch over recent years and the same will happen to other farms under which coal is worked. Before long the whole parish will suffer drought and be deprived of the springs that have gushed from its surface for thousands of years. Mark my words! We will soon have to build waterworks.'

At this juncture a strong breeze got up and rustled the branches of the trees, while the old yew looked as though it was about to move through the churchyard like a hearse. The Pistyll roared more noisily than ever as it bounded over the ridge. The owl hooted eerily from its hiding-place. Daearwynno dogs began barking and the Nantyrysfa dogs gave prompt reply. The sound penetrated the valley like something fearsome from a strange world, as I continued my walk alone in search of the sources of the old wells.

The spring that links the Lan and the Penrhiwceibr farmhouses has bubbled forth sweetly and clearly for ages. Always cheerful, she gave freely to all who sought her sustenance. Yet now, she has fallen into dire straights, like a lady once great in rank who has been brought to her knees. So poor is she that she cannot shed a tear of remembrance for the past and the transformation that has overtaken her.

Then again, there is the spring at Pentwyn Isaf. I remember it at all times of the year, flowing strongly and clearly. Neither poet nor prophet had ever thought of predicting its end. Yet now its vigour has ebbed away and it has died a death. Like a pilgrim, exhausted by climbing, it feels it is better to succumb. Soon the land that it has so richly watered for countless ages will be parched and what was the Well of Pentwyn will have vanished, never to attract the gaze of man or beast.

There is a spring, perhaps the fullest in the parish, which rises on the slopes of Ffynnondwym; the farm itself bears its name. It rises near the new rain-shelter, rushing mightily down the slope, a blessing to human and animal alike. I can now see myself bending to raise a handful of its pure, fresh water to my lips! Will this ever run dry? Will you ever stop flowing, you faithful maid, you who have given your services so freely and noiselessly for thousands of years? I fear that the coal-pit is greedy enough to swallow you whole, the black, greedy seducer!

Ffynnon y March (the Horse Spring) is on the roadside from Ynysybwl to Ffynnondwym. It gushes out from a small copse, just below the Hendre Ganol. At the height of summer it is as cold as ice and in the depth of winter it is so warm that it never freezes. There is a tradition connected with this spring about a certain horse that belonged to Ffynnondwym. It would drink only from this spring, and even if it were away at a fair or market, it would not touch a drop until it came back. On returning, it would always make for the spring in the copse near the house. Hence the name of the spring, Ffynnon y March.

Another well-known spring is Illtyd's Spring, which rushes from the shelter of the rocks at Buarth-y-Capel, never failing, whatever the season. Its source is in a grove of alders where the soil is wet and peaty. I remember my father taking me there when I was but three years old to hold my swollen ankle under the cold water. That was my first experience of real pain. The water was so icy as I tried to keep my foot under it, that pain and Ffynnon Illtyd have always been linked together in my mind. Despite this, my spirit has been eased a thousand times by this spring since that childhood experience. Often when I have been weary, a drink of this water given me by my mother has brought new life to the body. My first attempt at composing poetry was dedicated to this spring. It was a splendid theme too; Illtyd's spring with its crystal flow from the alder bushes, bounding out of the rock at Buarth y Capel to rush headlong on its mission to join the Ffrwd stream. I knew little of the Muse then, but this is what I wrote:

'Pure was the water in the earth, pure was the water in its flow,
But when it joined the River Ffrwd, it became a devil's brew.'

I have written many and better verses since then, most of which I have now forgotten. Still, the first lines I ever wrote under the big hazel tree in the swamp of Ffynnon Illtyd have left an indelible mark on my memory. I offer them, not as a sign of early talent, but as one's feeble attempts at awakening my literary ambitions. Dear old Ffynnon Illtyd,- never dry up! May the coal seams never impede your progress! Keep on flowing until the great flames of the Last Day drink you dry to immortality.

Higher up on the Ffrwd valley is the Fanheulog spring, which also runs into the Ffrwd. It is some distance from the farm but its water is like the finest wine flowing from the heart of the Coedcae. It runs out over a wooden spout on to a bed of stems and leaves all piled up in the whirlpool there. Then, off they all go through the wood to join the little river. Oh! How quiet is everything here. How gently does the water emerge from the Coedcae at Fanheulog. No noise, no shout; only a poetic whisper that would delight the heart of an angel. Thus it comes out from the shelter of thorns and hazel trees. Little of human toil is seen here; all is God's work - pure, unadulterated nature. How tragic that man should upset such peace as this. But I dread the day when I hear that the water of this spring is receding and that the voice from the depths has commanded it to appear in the dark land of coal, instead of sparkling in the clear air of Mynydd Gwyngul.

Higher up again, on the summit of the hill, is Llwynperdid, the house that was destroyed in the terrible fire early last summer. Near it is a strong spring coming out of the mountain, because the house and spring are at the top of the hill. It provides a strong current as it flows over the Coedcae to join the Cynin stream at Llysnant. Yet there are no signs of the collieries sapping the strength of the Llwynperdid spring!

We step across the narrow valley to the old mansion of the Glôg, near which, on the eastern side of the hill, the spring rushes forth. This is the spring of springs in Llanwynno. It comes out from the hillside with the energy of a waterfall, foaming white, and then flows over its stony bed, sparkling and shining enough to attract beings more pure than us, children of the earth, to drink from it.

When I suffered from a high temperature some years ago, I longed for its waters as did King David for the waters of the well of Bethlehem. Some of the water was brought to me to quench my great thirst, and its sweetness remains on my lips to this day. Oh! it would be a travesty of justice to stop the flow of this holy spring. It would be such a terrible loss if it were prevented from dancing its life away through the cracks in the Glôg hill. It would mean the loss of the water of angels! Yes, and so would a piece of poetry that only God could have created, be lost. Sadly, I fear the spring will soon be no more. Coal is being worked in the valley below and under the earth all round us. One can hardly expect a miracle, even one that saves the Glôg spring from the jaws of the miner. Yet it would be better to lose many entire islands than to lose this spring. I wish no harm to trade and industry; these things must be. I don't wish to criticise those who are risking their money in the pursuit of coal, and in so doing, destroying the landscape. I wish them all success, and success also to the brave miners who venture onto the bowels of the earth to retrieve the coal. Yet, through their ventures they are defacing my beloved country. They disturb the solitude, the quiet, poetic corners and suck dry the precious wells of my youth. This is why I weep and grieve!

CHAPTER
TWENTY EIGHT

MORE SPRINGS

I have named but few of the well-known springs in the parish. They were just like stars - clear landmarks, beautiful and useful, bubbling and sparkling over the wide face of the parish. By their different names they were as well-known as the hills. They were as close to us as to be regarded as fellow-parishioners! Here are some of them. The well at Cae-Cwar (Quarry Field), Gellilwch, hidden in the grass at the edge of the wood, seeming so bashful and demure, with water as cold as ice on an Alpine summit.

There was Ffynnon y Bwtri (The Buttery Well) in the house of Gellilwch. For years it had been there in grave solitude with no one ever hearing it as it bubbled up from the ground. Yet it came up forcefully and for many years it had been the source of water supply for the inhabitants of Gellilwch. However, having given its services free throughout the years, it had to flee from its old home and refrain from showing its modest face in the darkness of the buttery. It was exiled some time ago, but like all good things, surely will not be irretrievably lost.

Where is the source of the Gellidawel spring near the Berw

(waterfall) of the Taff? People years ago put much faith in its virtues. I recall, when I was young, listening to old Evan Rosser and Sally talking about it. The conversation went along these lines.

'Well, Rosser, where are you off to today?'

'I am off to the Gellidawel spring to bathe my eyes, if you must know my business.'

'There's no *must* about it, since an honest man need not be afraid of saying what he is about.'

'I don't know that an honest man does want to know everybody's business,' retorted Rosser angrily, as he continued his tramp towards the spring.

On the way back the two met again and Sally began,

'Do you think that the virtues of that spring are any better than those of other springs, Rosser?'

'I don't *think*, I know from experience, and whoever says otherwise is a liar' replied Rosser. The sparks were beginning to fly again!

Oh! Well,' said Sally, 'why do you judge that this water excels over any other?'

'Oh! It has surely bestowed a greater blessing; or perhaps some angel has influenced it for good like the one at the Pool of Bethesda, for all we know.'

'Nonsense! I will never believe that God has blessed some water more than another,' said Sally.

'Perhaps you do not believe in anything,' answered Rosser. 'I don't suppose you believe that God has created any human being different from another, although here you are breaking up stones by the yard while I am a gentleman and commended by the parish.'

Off went Rosser towards Pontypridd, while Sally's hammer sounded 'thump, thump' on the stones.

But where is that spring now? Does it still rise as it once did among the grass and rushes to be lost in the Taff, even as Time itself is lost in distant Eternity?

Then we have the well at the Cefn, which once flowed freely as if a spirit below the ground from Graig-yr-Hesg had been ordered to work the pump in order to bring a flood of pure water for the men and animals of the Cefn. I remember one of the Cefn maids being badly frightened at the well on one occasion. She ran back to the house and called on Mr Walters, the master at that time, better known as Tommy the Cefn.

'Come at once to the well,' she said, 'there's a big snake there with horns in its head. Come quickly.'

'What is the matter, girl?' he said, 'You must be off your head. Who ever saw a snake with horns?'

Tommy went to the well and there indeed was a big snake, which at first sight appeared to have two horns. But, on closer inspection he saw that the snake had tried to swallow a large frog that had got stuck in its throat, leaving two legs protruding from the jaw, giving the appearance of horns. The snake had bitten off more than it could chew! I don't know whether an incident of this kind gave rise to a proverb often heard in the parish in times gone by, 'Never try to swallow a frog'.

Another fine spring is Ffynnon Nicholas in Penparc Wood. It flows strongly and I believe that the water from it comes out by Tŷ'r Twyn at the Basin (Abercynon), to feed the Taff Vale Railway engines. Those who hunt and shoot know about the spring and if there are any woodcock in the area, you'll find them near Ffynnon Nicholas, or as some of the old people call it, 'the Spring of the Woodcocks.'

Then again, we have Tydraw well near Cwmclydach. Here Evan Morgan and Maggie drew their water, believing that none purer came through the earth's crust. Today, however, it is no more. The New Bridge put an end to it. And the place from where it came knows nothing of its existence. Nevertheless Ffynnon Caban still runs in the Cyll y Cwm Wood (Hazel Wood). It is feeble but as pure and constant as nature itself. Many of the residents of Cwmclydach drank from it, although it is now but a trickle.

To the men of the hills Ffynnon Dyllgoed is well-known. Its source is near Penrhiw gate, at the lower end of the road leading from Ynyshir to Mynydd Gwyngul in the direction of Llanwynno. Before you leave the road for the mountain, you come across this fine spring. It rushes out from the bowels of the earth, from the underground reservoir of Mynydd Gwyngul, and runs through the fields to the Rhondda Fach River. One does not often see such a strong flow of clear, sparkling water coming out of a round hole in the earth. There is neither house nor pig-sty anywhere near, except for Penrhiw which shelters in the wood lower down the road. This dwelling takes its name from the well - Rhiw Ffynnon Dyllgoed. Apart from an occasional walker crossing the bank on the hill and sitting there to quench his thirst at the spring, there is nothing to be seen on its banks but bushes, grass and rushes, with an occasional visit from birds from Penrhiw Wood or the lapwings of Mynydd Gwyngul. The old spring still flows through rushes, grass and brambles, and like Time itself, is never-ceasing. May it flow for ever! Oh! how dear, how delectable, how romantic! What ode or poem ever composed was to be compared with this one? This is one of God's own. The bards can sit to read and study it, and so recognise their own limitations! Oh! my little ones! Create a spring if you can. Only then will you have something to boast about!

It is difficult to pass this spring without mentioning Tommy Penrhiw. Everybody knew him and the old mare that he always led by the halter. I never saw a bridle in his hand, only that rope on the mare's head. You would see Tommy pulling forward and the mare partly resisting, so that their halting progress provided much amusement to onlookers. I can only recall Tommy being on the mare's back twice. One occasion was when the old mare slipped into a ditch on the hill above Buarth y Capel and Tommy fell into a pool of peaty water. What a performance there was! Tommy was wearing a round, hard-wearing jacket to the waist and a pair of corduroy trousers, recently washed. As he fell, Tommy's braces gave way. What a sight he was, struggling towards the smithy, holding up his trousers with one hand and pulling the mare with the other, while between his teeth was a short, black pipe, almost empty of tobacco and no light in it, until he reached his good friend, Will the Blacksmith. It was left to Will to help repair the pipe and the trousers, as well as the old mare's shoes!

Tommy lived in Penrhiw for many years. I don't suppose he liked anything better than taking the old mare to the smithy at Ynysybwl to have a chat with Will. I am doubtful whether Tommy saw anything poetic about the Dyllgoed spring! No, he saw nothing more than the beauty that can be found anywhere. It is not likely that the murmur and babble of this sparkling spring ever thrilled him, despite having lived on its brink for so long, quietly and harmlessly enough. Yes, the spring flows along still, but Tommy lies in the City of those who have passed to their rest where I hope he has recognised a better spring than the Dyllgoed - a spring that has cleansed the house of David and the people of Jerusalem 'as white as the snow in Zalmon,' as the Psalmist puts it.

It's strange not to hear of a Holy Well in the parish, for where there were monks and a monastery one usually found a Holy Well, Mary's Well, or the Virgin's Well. Mary's Well (or the Shrine of Our Lady, as it is called) is still to be found on the slopes of Penrhys, facing the Ystrad (Rhondda Fawr) Valley, although the monastery and the monks' graves have long since disappeared. In Holywell, North Wales, Gwenfrewi, or Winifred's Well, is still well-known near St Asaph. Indeed not far from where I am writing, stands an old church known formerly as Capel Eglwys Mair (the Chapel of Mary's Church). The building is now in ruins, but the well - Mary's Well - is still in full flow. It is therefore surprising that no well of that religious connection is to be found in Llanwynno. Usually the monks were wise, knowledgeable people who understood nature and her secrets. It would not take them long to find a source of pure, health-giving water wherever they went. They were aware that minerals had an effect on the water and on all who drank it. Thus they placed the beneficial effects of the water under the protection of the Holy Virgin. Hence we have the name of the well and thus every Mary's Well became a holy well.

But the fact remains- Where is the Mary's Well of Llanwynno? Didn't they have a holy well in the parish? I believe there was one, but the name and the tradition have become lost, as happens sometimes. Perhaps there had grown in the parish strong opposition to Roman Catholicism. This could have led to a successful attempt to do away with anything that savoured of Popery. Thus the Virgin's Well may have lost its name, and in the course of a generation or two, both the well and its location would have been lost, even to local tradition. There is the farm above Graigwen called Gellifynaches (Nun's Grove), it's true, but no trace of a well is to be seen in the vicinity.

[Interestingly, the name 'Nun's Crescent' is given to one of the streets on the housing estate that stands today at the top of Graigwen – author]

There is a very fine spring near Mynachdy even to this day. It rises in the corner of the field called Fanheulog and runs round the neck of the valley to a large water chute at the farthest end of Mynachdy garden. It is strong and clear and sometimes I was inclined to think that this may have been the Holy Well, and that it was here that the monks washed during their happy stay in the parish. But having looked and pondered the matter, I have come to the conclusion that this was not the Holy Well, despite the fact that the water may have been holy in the eyes of the monks. It is most likely on reflection that Gwynno's Well, near the church, was the Holy Well. It rises below the ridge of the church and, I believe, possessed great properties. It will be remembered that Roman Catholics always built their churches near a spring or well which afterwards became consecrated. In this case it was not called after the name of the Virgin Mary, but dedicated to the guardian of the parish, Saint Gwynno, after whom it has ever since been named. It flows quietly from below the church and its water is as pure and clear as any in the land. Llanwynno beer should be pure if it is produced from the water of Gwynno's well! Not that he, poor soul, had been responsible for its qualities, for that spring, as the poet said, is the work of God himself.

'This spring is the crystal wine of the Creator, a perfect beverage; At summer's height, there's plenty to drink, God's vessel supplies the water.'

CHAPTER
TWENTY NINE

THE OLD CHAPEL

The two houses on the hillock a little above the new Calvinistic Methodist chapel in Llanwynno still retain an air of sanctity. The reason can be explained by the fact that they constituted the original chapel. This was the place of worship, the temple, the house of prayer which served many generations of worshippers, though never consecrated by a bishop nor designed by any noteworthy builder. In fact its only adornment was a coat of whitewash once a year on the walls, a little dark-blue paint at the corners, and occasionally some mortar between the grey stones, just to keep the place water-tight. The interior walls were bare, except for the clock in front of the pulpit and a row of long nails along the side walls and the back, on which men hung their hats.

Like the exterior, the inside walls were white-washed. There was a row of seats along the back wall from end to end that faced the pulpit, another row along the eastern wall and from the east door to the pulpit steps, and from the other side of the pulpit to the far door as far as the fire-place. In a word, the seats were firmly fixed with their backs to the wall, the Big Seat in the centre, together with two small seats, one on either side of the Big Seat. The seats bore no numbers but were known by the names of families in the parish, such as Mynachdy seat, Glôg seat and Fanheulog seat. There was also a bench with arms and back to it on which people could sit back to back. This was at the eastern end, opposite the door. Then there was a rather long bench on the middle of the floor opposite the Big Seat and two other benches facing each other on either side of the fireplace. There was also a fixed bench around and outside the Big Seat and those who sat on it had their backs to the Big Seat and the pulpit. This was a good place for those who did not want to face the preacher, but for those who wished to listen in comfort it was purgatory!

There were three windows at one end, the pulpit being opposite the middle one. In fact the inside sill was the pulpit seat. The pulpit therefore was right in the middle of the chapel, facing the north wall with its row of seats and the clock, which was presented to the chapel in my time, situated meaningfully right opposite the pulpit on the plain white-washed wall. At the back of the chapel there is a stone tablet in the wall stating that the chapel was built in 1786. The cost was borne by the members and their friends, and although it could not be said to be a handsome building, there were signs that the Spirit of God was with the people there and had blessed them with a beauty greater than that of grand architecture and fine walls, namely, the sanctification of souls. There was fervour in this chapel and at many of its services 'the living Spirit was felt.'

I have heard voices uplifted in song and praise hundreds of times between the walls of the old Fanheulog Chapel. Many giants of the ministry preached here, pleading the forgiveness of sins through the blood of Jesus Christ. God was with them, strengthening and encouraging them, helping to make the place 'a house of God and a gateway to Heaven'. Many souls were saved. There are many pilgrims safe in Paradise tonight who began their spiritual journey in the plain little chapel of Llanwynno. Their names may be forgotten here, but they are securely enrolled in the Book of Life.

Oh! You holy pilgrims of Llanwynno, reproved, nurtured and fortified in the old chapel until you became strong to follow the steps of your Saviour and have proved that 'God deals gently', and have felt the dew and spiritual rain descend upon your souls. You have rejoiced like those who have received a great reward and have sung in your zealous, rustic manner, your voices raised, knowing little of the rules of music and poetry, yet following the dictates of something higher. When your spirits have softened under the influence of Spirit of Truth, you have sung not once, twice, or three times, but a hundred times the words of the old hymn, 'Mi gana am waed yr Oen' ('I sing of the blood of the Lamb'), until the walls and the roof of the old chapel on the hill have shaken to the resounding echoes.

Yes! You sang a great deal and the echoes have settled in the rock of Cae Tŷ Cwrdd (Chapel House Field). I would have liked to have had your names to list them here. I would have recorded every one with great pleasure from the founding of the chapel to the departure of the last members of Llanwynno Chapel. Sadly such a list is not in my possession. However, all the names are chronicled in the Book of the Lamb! If ever I reach that heavenly country, I will come and shake you by the hand, to talk of the happy old times and to learn the names of those of my old parish who 'on their hands and feet tried to reach the heights.'

By today, the old chapel has been converted into two dwelling-houses, but somehow I can only visualise it as a chapel. It is a pity that it could not have been kept as it was with the old pulpit-chair put back in its place as it was a hundred and one years ago and for many years afterwards. Yet it is pointless speaking in this vein. The one-time temple has been turned into a dwelling-place. The new chapel stands on a parcel of land belonging to the old chapel. The 'New House' is located where Richard and Maggie Williams had their garden. May the new chapel be as spiritually fruitful as the garden was fruitful by nature, when Maggie gathered her various crops each year over a long period.

Hywel Harris (of Methodist Revival fame) preached in Llanwynno before the Old Chapel was built. The services were held at Rhydygwreiddyn, Pwllhelyg and Tŷ-tan-wal, near Mynachdy. There is no doubt that in one of these farms Hywel Harris delivered powerful sermons, as did the immortal Jones of Llangan. According to the periodical 'Methodistiaeth Cymru' (Welsh Methodism), in the year 1774 the faithful met in a house known as Tŷ-tan-wal (the House under the Wall) and they witnessed to clear signs of God's presence among them, 'when at times they would begin to praise God with loud cries.' It is on record that John Evans of Cilycwm was preaching there on one occasion, taking his text from the prophet Ezra Chapter 3 verse 13, 'For the people shouted with a loud shout and the noise was heard afar off.' In this meeting some people fainted with fear, others wept and some sang in praise. When the congregation met at Tŷ-tan-wal, it was said to have numbered from 30 to 45.

It is clear that even in those days the people of Llanwynno were emotional in their way of worshipping, as they are today. It would be interesting to know the names of those who fainted, wept and sang, but the chronicler named no-one. As I said, I regret not having a list of these old residents, but I can remember some of them and so can many other people. Janet Thomas Howell, who died over thirty years ago, was someone remembered for her enthusiasm for religion. She was an old lady of strong common-sense, not easily carried away with her feelings, but even she would respond with fervour and thanksgiving on occasions. Her religious spirit was revealed most deeply in her own home, in the way in which she read a chapter of the Bible all alone and in the prayers she offered each night and morning. Janet was one of the true saints of Llanwynno.

Griffiths of Glyncoch and Evans of Daearwynno were also noted for their godliness and zeal, but they had crossed the river before my time. They were among those Methodists who would take Communion only in the parish church. For years after the chapel was built the members would attend Llanwynno church for Communion at the hands of the vicar.

I also remember Ifan Rhys with his gentle prayer, his charming voice and tender sayings; he was a sweet singer and often gave out this hymn: *Let the sharp, keen breezes blow o'er new Jerusalem's hill and let my inward heart rejoice*

He often attended the monthly meeting at Pyle on behalf of the church. The first meeting of the year was always held there since its establishment by Jones of Llangan in honour of old William Thomas of Pyle. He was entreated to speak in the meeting and was greatly encouraged by those present. However Ifan was of the opinion that there had already been more than sufficient talking, and of a high standard too, so he felt constrained not to add anything. But the chairman insisted on his saying something.

'Come, come, brother of Llanwynno,' he said, 'say something, if it's only a word.' Ifan rose and said, 'Amen' with great passion, and sat down. It gave him great pleasure to think that no one was bored with the speech of the delegate from Llanwynno. Ifan Rhys has gone to the 'gathering of the first born' these many years.

Another character that writes itself on my memory in connection with the old chapel was Joseph Davies, the old schoolmaster there and a powerful man in public prayer and a very good reader. Perhaps he was ahead of his time and on this account his talents may not have been appreciated as they should have been. I remember him sitting in his usual place under the pulpit. Whenever there was a robust preacher above him expounding a resounding challenge in his message, one would see two streams of tears on his cheeks. As the 'hwyl' (passion) of the preacher increased and the response of the congregation deepened, Joseph would sway to and fro, as if his spirit had been thoroughly shattered. As a child I recall seeing Joseph weeping during a sermon, delivered by Edward Matthews of Ewenny. I thought at the time that I had never seen such enormous tears; they were just like large peas. Mr Matthews must have preached a very gripping sermon on this particular occasion. For some time now Joseph had been swaying like a young branch in the wind and had dared to get to his feet to look over the ledge of the pulpit - a sure sign that things were 'warming up'. The tears rolled down his cheeks in an unceasing flood. At last the preacher reached the climax of his exposition. He now pictures the meeting of two seas. He relates:

'A ship happens to be approaching this strange meeting-place of the two seas, where all is turmoil. The enormous waves like huge mountains are rolling to meet each other; spume and mist are rising

from the terrible abyss, while the noise is like the shattering of worlds. Yes, the awful abyss opens out like eternity and the ship goes down from the angry crest of one of the tempestuous waves to vanish out of sight into the whirling depths-out of reach of any help, out of sight of even hope itself! No! Some secret power throws the ship out of the dreadful turmoil of the two seas to land on its keel safe and sound in calm water out of range of all storm and tempest! It is the soul being taken from the body, the dead being released from the storm of death in the meeting of the two seas! It is sinking! Down it went! No! Heaven's blessing! 'The eternal arms are supporting you.' The ship is carried across the awe-inspiring abyss of the meeting-place. The waters are stilled. The peaceful haven has been reached!

I can recall no more of the address, except for Joseph's shout at the end! Oh! Dear Heaven, what a shout! And what tears! When the ship reached the safety of the quiet water, I felt that Joseph was also lifted from where he stood. He felt his soul being lifted above the breakers, above the storm, above all peril, to the rock that will stand firm in the Last Day. As he uttered those joyful words, 'Alleluia! Alleluia! Thanks be to God,' Joseph called to mind the lines of the hymn,

'This is the rock which stands in the sea, the firmest rock that ever stood; When in trouble, it will banish all fear from my heart.'

Maggie Williams took up the theme of the same hymn, raising her voice in triumph. Before Maggie had finished, Mrs Davies of Tynewydd had begun to sing at the other end of the seat. Last of all, the spirit of George Davies was ignited and he uttered one loud shout - the loudest I ever heard from his lips - 'Thanks everlasting!' With that, I thought that the Quarry and the Gelynog Wood answered the shout, retaining the echoes. It is still ringing in my ears!

Another in the list of pilgrims was Evan Davies from Penrhys. He was not gifted with regard to eloquence; his prayers were brief. Yet he was like a lump of gold and his faith came from the heart. Although unable to pour out his heart in a fluent outpouring of emotion to stir those who listened, he nevertheless reminded them all that he was talking to the Father, and he apologised for nothing, nor did he ask for anything but what he truly felt. He travelled twice a week for many years from Penrhys, near Ystradyfodwg, over Mynydd Gwyngul, to the chapel at Llanwynno. He passed away about seventeen years ago. Having suffered a long illness, his arrival at the shore where there is no pain was sweet.

Titus Jones, despite his eccentricities, also deserves mention as a member of this family of faith. He lived in Llanwynno for years. I remember well the incident when he put the house alight by setting fire to a heap of wood and straw so that the children in his care should have an idea of what Hell was like! He was the strangest preacher who ever to grace a pulpit. I heard him mention in a sermon dealing with the evils of smoking tobacco, 'If the Good Lord had intended you to smoke, he would have put a flue at the top of your head.' And on another occasion he declared, 'The devil is like the gander at the Mill; if you run away, he'll follow you and cause you harm, but if you turn and face him, he'll run away quickly enough, the coward!'

His voice rose on the last sentence into the most unrefined voice I have ever heard. It was a sort of squeaky tenor. Whenever he shouted, as he often did, the effect was most offensive to the ears. He was foolish enough to get married in his old age and the marriage proved a failure. He had announced in the Monthly

Meeting that he was soon going to wed, amid smiles and laughter from those present. The Reverend David Roberts of Cowbridge, as chairman, tried to persuade him to think things over and remain in his current status, giving strong reasons for his point of view. Titus in reply appealed to the meeting, causing much laughter in the process by saying, 'Look, he (that is, David Roberts) has had four wives and he is not willing to let me have one.' This was quite true. Mr Roberts had just been married for the fourth time and his widow is now the wife of the old patriarch, Mr Evans of Tonyrefail, who is rapidly nearing his century! – which only proves the theory, 'It's never too late!'.

In spite of being so unconventional, Titus was a man of God and, for all his slovenliness and eccentricity, it was felt that he feared God. There was every reason to believe that Heaven had blessed his unorthodox sermons as a means of saving sinners. Mr Matthews collected money to support him in his old age, since many unscrupulous people had borrowed from him without his obtaining receipts for the money, with the result that he lost practically all he had. Sadly, he ended his days in the workhouse.

I have previously mentioned the names of Rachel Jones of the Cwm and George Davies and Ann. Rachel, the daughter of old Rhys Phylip, was quiet, faithful and godly throughout her life. Rhys Phylip was my great grandfather. He had joined the saints in song on 'the other side' before I was born, but his name, his sayings, his zeal and his godliness are still remembered in the parish. George Davies and his wife were pillars of the congregation for many years. They had much of this world's goods which they used in order to foster the cause of the Lord in the parish. Mr Davies died ripe in years. Leaving the old chapel was hard for him as he had spent his life there in the worship of God. However he contributed substantially towards the cost of the new chapel and lived to see it completed. Then he took to his bed and departed from this world in peace.

And now I turn aside and take off my hat as I kneel humbly to show my love, my respect and my affection for the sacred old land of Gwynno, the parish of my birth, the beloved playground of my childhood, and the place of sleep of a host of friends and relations.